Dedication

This book is dedicated to the surgeons, doctors and nursing staff of the Neo-natal Unit of Alder Hey Children's Hospital, Liverpool, without whom this story could not have been told.

"In order to write one's reminiscences it is not at all necessary to be a great man, nor a notorious criminal, nor a celebrated artist, nor a statesman - it is quite enough to be simply a human being, to have something to tell, and not merely the desire to tell it but at least have some little ability to do so."

Alexander Herzen.

Author's Note

I began writing this book many years after the events described took place and, although I have an excellent memory, the dialogue contained in these pages is my recollection of the tone and substance of the conversations that took place and may not be verbatim. Also, after so many years have gone by, my memory of the names of the cast of characters may be flawed and, if I have got them wrong, I sincerely apologise to the individuals concerned. However, I am confident that the names of the principal participants of this story are accurate.

My descriptions of the medical conditions, which are an essential part of this story, are not attributable to any medical textbook and I have received no training that would qualify me to offer an opinion in these matters. For authenticity, I first relied on my memory and then researched the conditions to make sure that there were no obvious "howlers". In talking this approach, my intention was to present the conditions as I remember them being described to me. Therefore, any errors or omissions are mine alone.

This book is principally about how my daughter, Karen, in particular, and we as a family, managed the debilitating condition of spina bifida. In my experience, no two spina bifida sufferers have the same degree of disability. Some can walk with crutches and may be doubly incontinent. Others may not be able to stand at all but may have full control of their bladder and bowels. The way I understand it, the level of disability can be severely exacerbated depending on the amount of trauma to the spinal cord – the "neural highway" – occurring during the birth process. So, if other spina bifida sufferers don't recognise the symptoms or conditions described in these pages, that is entirely to be expected.

David L Verinder

July, 2018.

One

I picked up on the first ring. "Hello," my sleep-deprived voice croaked.

"Mr Verinder?"

"Yes."

"Hello. This is Sister O'Hara at Sefton General Hospital." The alluring Galway accent reminded me of Maureen O'Hara in *The Quiet Man*. I imagined the fresh-complexioned features of the famous actress, a vision of wholesome beauty. Who better to deliver the joyous news I had been expecting for the past eight hours than her namesake? "Your wife has had a baby girl."

My heart performed a drum roll. I covered the mouthpiece and shouted, "Mum, it's a girl!" My mother, brothers and sisters were upstairs in bed, but I knew Mum would be restless, waiting for news of her first grandchild.

The charming Irish voice cut in. "Mr Verinder, I'm afraid there's a problem."

"What do you mean?" I heard my voice quiver. "Is my wife okay?"

"Don't be alarmed. Your wife is fine. However, there's a problem with the baby's back, and the doctor would like to talk with you about it."

"What kind of problem?"

"Mr Verinder, it really would be better if the doctor explained this to you in person. Please come to the hospital as soon as you can."

"Okay, I'll be there in 20 minutes." I grabbed my car keys and headed for the door. Reaching for the latch, I glanced up the stairs. Mum was half-way down, knotting the belt of her dressing gown. "Mum, there's something wrong with the baby. I have to go to the hospital." She paused, holding onto the banister, frowning. I ran down the garden path to my battered Ford Prefect.

Mum had reached the front door. "What's wrong with her? D'you want me to come with you?" she shouted, but I was already in the car.

I wound the window down and yelled, "I'll call you later."

I pulled out the choke and hit the starter button. The engine started immediately but stalled as I engaged first gear. The old car was temperamental, but I could live with the inconvenience considering it had cost me just ten pounds—half my monthly earnings. I pressed the starter button again; the engine turned over, caught, then died. *Shit! Come on, for God's sake!* I tried again and this time it sputtered into life. I floored the accelerator and the engine roared. I crunched the gearshift lever into first and sped off down the street. Glancing in the rear-view mirror through hazy exhaust fumes, I saw Mum at the garden gate. She fidgeted with the collar of her dressing gown.

As I drove, I replayed the conversation with Sister O'Hara in my mind.

What could be wrong with the baby's back? Every new-born I had ever known had been just perfect. Faces like prunes, but perfect in every other way. Maybe it's a birthmark? Or perhaps a mole? What else could it be? What if her spine is deformed? No! Think positive thoughts. Rita is okay, and the baby will be fine, too. My very own daughter! Carole-Ann! If she looked like her mother, she would be blessed. If she looked like me… well, I hoped she hadn't inherited my nose.

-0-0-0-0-0-

Sister O'Hara looked nothing like the illustrious actress of the same name. She was tiny, gaunt, a nun without a habit, but with a voice that would melt glacial ice. She took my arm and guided me into her office at the entrance to the maternity ward. "Mr Verinder, please have a seat. Dr Wilson will see you shortly."

I sat on a moulded plastic chair in front of a grey metal desk, cluttered with papers, folders, charts, and small plastic sample tubes. Sister O'Hara sat on a swivel-chair behind the desk. I looked into her eyes, seeking a sign the problem was minor, finding none. My voice was unsteady, as questions tumbled from my lips. "When can I see my wife? And the baby? What's the problem? Is it serious?"

"Please, Mr Verinder, the doctor will explain everything. He's examining your daughter now and he'll be here soon. Karen is a lovely name. Is she named after anyone?"

"Karen? Her name's not Karen. We're calling our daughter Carole-Ann."

"But your wife told the hospital chaplain your daughter's name was Karen."

The chaplain? Why had the chaplain been there? It suddenly hit me. He must have been called to baptise the baby or to administer the Anglican equivalent of the last rites.

The door opened and a young white-coated doctor came in. "Mr Verinder, I'm Dr Wilson, Consultant Gynaecologist."

He had fair hair, a blonde moustache and a contralto voice. We shook hands and he sat next to me on a similar grey, plastic chair, which complemented the drab indexed filing cabinets lined up on the far wall.

Sister O'Hara got up from her desk and excused herself.

Dr Wilson had shining aquamarine eyes, which peered at me with a mixture of sympathy and, I guessed, disbelief at my youthful appearance. I was twenty-years-old but was often asked if I was over eighteen by wary pub landlords. He leaned toward me, clasping his hands over his knees. His face was solemn. "Your daughter has a condition called *spina bifida*," he began. "This is not my specialty, and there's very little I can tell you, other than her spine hasn't formed properly, and part of the spinal cord is exposed through a break in the skin on her lower back. Unfortunately, Karen was born in the breach position, bottom first, and this has almost certainly caused some damage to the exposed area of the spinal cord."

"Her name is Carole-Ann, not Karen."

He continued as though I hadn't spoken. "Your daughter needs surgery to repair the damage, and it must be performed as soon as possible. Fortunately, the neo-natal unit at Alder Hey Children's Hospital has a team of specialists qualified to treat this condition. The unit is one of the best facilities in the country, and they have been very successful in treating spina bifida."

My head drooped and a maelstrom of questions whirled through my brain. I had read stories of deformed or disabled babies in magazines like Reveille and Readers Digest, but this kind of thing simply didn't happen to me or my family. Rita and I had such grand plans for our baby daughter. She was going to be a dancer, a great ballerina.

I looked up and Dr Wilson's piercing blue eyes scrutinised my face. It wasn't a bad dream. This really was happening to me. And, more importantly, it was happening to my baby. "What causes spina bifida?" I asked.

"We're not sure. It results from the failure of the spine to form properly during the first month of pregnancy. Surgery to close the open wound on the back is normally performed within twenty-four hours of birth to minimise the risk of infection, and to preserve any existing function in the spinal cord."

"Will she be okay?"

"If she's treated immediately, she has a chance. We must get her to

Alder Hey as soon as possible, and it would be best if you went with her. Sister O'Hara is arranging this as we speak."

"Does my wife know?"

"We've told her there's a problem with the baby's back, but she's still drowsy from the sedative we gave her immediately after the birth."

Sister O'Hara knocked on the glass partition and came in carrying a tiny bundle wrapped in a white shawl. "Here's your daughter, Mr Verinder," she said, handing her to me. "I'm sorry, but the chaplain has baptised her *Karen*, as instructed by your wife. An ambulance is waiting outside to take you to Alder Hey. I'll walk with you."

I cradled the baby, uncertain how to hold her, afraid I might hurt her. She was pink and wrinkled, with a little button nose and mewling lips. She was gorgeous and she was mine.

"Good luck, Mr Verinder," said Dr Wilson, as we left the office.

On the way down the long, green-walled corridor, Sister O'Hara explained it was standard hospital procedure to baptise children born with this kind of condition. The chaplain had misheard Rita and thought the baby was to be called Karen.

"Then *Karen* it shall be," I said, kissing her on the forehead. She looked just like any other new-born. I almost convinced myself there was nothing wrong, but the waiting ambulance, blue light flashing, reminded me of the seriousness of her condition. I said goodbye to Sister O'Hara.

She patted my arm. "God bless you. I'll pray for your daughter."

The ambulance sped away, bell clanging, on its five-mile journey to Alder Hey.

-0-0-0-0-0-

The male ambulance attendant told me Alder Hey had a first-class reputation for the treatment of *spina bifida*, and babies with this condition were routinely brought to the neo-natal unit from all over England. I heard him, but I wasn't paying attention. I was fascinated by the puckered face peeping out from the shawl. She gripped my finger so tightly it started to tingle. A flood of love filled my heart. *Please, God, keep her safe.*

A few minutes later, the ambulance turned into the landscaped driveway of Alder Hey Children's Hospital. A brass plaque, set into a sandstone arch at the entrance, informed visitors the hospital had been opened in 1914. The ambulance attendant escorted me and my baby along the central corridor, which was almost deserted on this Sunday morning. We passed the Radiology and Out-Patients departments and took the lift to the second floor.

Karen whimpered and stirred in my arms, as we followed signs directing us past the J, K, L, and M orthopaedic wards to the neo-natal unit at the end of the corridor. Double doors adjacent to the unit led to operating theatres.

At the entrance to the unit, a nurse took Karen, and asked me to remain in the waiting room while the doctors examined her. The ambulance attendant shook my hand. "Good luck. I hope she'll be okay."

"Thanks a lot."

He left me alone.

I rubbed my arms, felt the fading warmth of my daughter's body heat and, already, I missed her special, new-born smell—a mixture of milk, talcum and soft baby skin. In the short time I'd held her, I realised we'd formed a bond that could never be broken. No matter what happened, whatever the prognosis, no one could take that away from us.

I could hear bleeps and gushes of air in the background, as I flicked through the pages of the *News of the World*, abandoned by a previous visitor. After what seemed like hours, but was probably only twenty minutes, a white coat and stethoscope appeared in my peripheral vision, and a tired male voice enquired, "Mr Verinder?"

I looked up, nodded, and grasped the outstretched hand.

He was tall, with dark curly hair, greying at the temples, and his fleshy face glistened with sweat. "My name is Peter Rickman. I'm a paediatric surgeon attached to the neo-natal unit. Let's go somewhere we can talk privately."

I followed him along a central corridor, rooms on either side containing incubators, tiny babies clearly visible. He paused outside the empty ward-sister's office, ushered me inside, and asked me to sit. He sat on the edge of the desk. "Mr Verinder, you already know your daughter has *spina bifida* and I will try to explain in simple terms what this condition is, how we can treat it, and what the likely prognosis is for your child's future."

I nodded, wanting to hear what he would say, but afraid of the connotations.

"*Spina bifida* is a Latin term meaning, literally, split spine," said Mr Rickman. "The central nervous system and backbone develop early in pregnancy, and *spina bifida* occurs when one or more vertebrae fail to develop fully, leaving a gap and exposing the spinal cord. In your daughter's case, this has occurred in the lower back, approximately at waist level."

"Is her spinal cord damaged?"

He paused, took a long breath, squeezed my arm. "Your daughter has the most serious form of *spina bifida*, called *myelomeningocele*. The spinal cord is damaged, and there is some paralysis below the damaged area."

"Will she be able to walk... when she grows up?" My voice trembled.

"It's too early to say, but it's very unlikely that your daughter will ever be able to walk. Movement depends on unobstructed nerve pathways from the brain and, in Karen's case, the pathways that control leg movement are partially blocked."

This was distressing, crushing, but he wasn't finished. He shifted his position and leaned closer. "There's a further complication. Your daughter has a related condition called *hydrocephalus*—an accumulation of cerebro-spinal fluid, or CSF, in the brain cavities. CSF is produced constantly inside the brain, flowing from one ventricle to the next and down the spinal column. CSF is normally re-circulated through the bloodstream but, if the pathways are blocked or over-production of CSF occurs, fluid accumulates in the skull and compresses the surrounding brain tissue."

My breathing became ragged. I lowered my head. "Jesus Christ," I wheezed.

"There's no easy way to say this." His expression was grave, and he gripped my arm with long, slender fingers. "Your daughter will die if we do not treat both the *spina bifida* and *hydrocephalus* within the next few hours."

His staccato words hit me like a burst from a machine gun. I looked around the spartan office, with its familiar grey, metal desk and filing cabinets, and ubiquitous plastic chairs, trying to gather my thoughts. "How will you treat her?" My voice sounded disconnected, as if it belonged to someone else.

"We must operate immediately to repair the lower back area and close the wound. This will protect the spinal cord from any further damage and will help to prevent infections such as *meningitis*."

The mention of *meningitis* filled me with dread, for a boyhood friend and near neighbour of mine, Brian Wilding, had died from *meningitis* in his late teens.

"Next, we will insert a valve through her skull to allow the excess CSF to flow through a tube back into the circulatory system via the heart. If the valve is not implanted, the build-up of pressure will result in brain damage and could cause blindness."

I grimaced and shook my head. Oh, my Lord above! They were going to operate on my daughter's brain, heart and spine and she was only a few hours old! How could a new-born possibly survive this trauma? A thousand questions swirled and bubbled in my mind. *Would she survive surgery? Would she be able to walk and talk like normal little girls? Would she be brain-damaged? What other problems might there be later? How would we manage? How could this happen to my child?*

Mr Rickman waited for the immediate shock to subside. "Mr Verinder, you have to make a very important decision, and I want you to think carefully about your answer. We have two choices. One is to do nothing for Karen and let nature take its course, and the other is to perform immediate surgery and try to save her."

His words hit me like a lightning bolt. *I was being asked to play God with my daughter's life!* "Mr Rickman," I said hoarsely, lower-lip trembling. "You must do everything in your power to save her…"

"Please think about it."

"I don't need to think about it." My voice had taken on a strong, aggressive tone. "You *must* operate."

"But, you don't understand." His voice was conciliatory. "Assuming she survives, which is by no means certain, she faces a life in and out of hospital. You face a very harrowing future looking after her. Please think about it carefully before deciding."

My tone softened. "I *have* thought about it and I want you to treat her… *please.*"

He sighed, relented. "We'll do all we can. Would you like to see your daughter before we prepare her for surgery?"

I nodded, unable to trust my voice, and he led me to a room opposite, where Karen lay in an incubator. She was awake, her lips pursed, searching for the sustenance of her mother's milk. She had thin auburn hair with a red hue, and she moved the fingers of one hand as if she were waving to me.

How could she be suffering from these horrific conditions, yet still look so… normal?

Mr Rickman came back into the room. "We'll need to get her ready now. The surgery will take about five hours, so I suggest you go home and come back this evening at visiting time. I'll let you know then how the surgery went and answer any further questions you may have."

I stood and blew Karen a kiss through the glass. A teardrop rolled down my cheek and I swiped it away. I was trying so hard to digest this appalling situation without falling apart, but my emotions were becoming frayed.

Mr Rickman shook my hand, held it for a beat. "Try not to worry, we'll do our best for her."

I walked out the door without turning back. Outside the neo-natal unit, I paused for a moment. The opening lines of the Beatles' song *I Saw Her*

Standing There, released a couple of years previously, came into my mind.

She was just seventeen, you know what I mean,

And the way she looked was way beyond compare…

My wife, Rita, who lay in a bed in Sefton General Hospital maternity ward, was just seventeen years old, and I was still two months away from my twenty-first birthday.

Retracing my steps through Alder Hey's labyrinth of corridors, I stopped at a pay phone near the entrance, and phoned the maternity ward to check on my wife. Sister O'Hara answered. "Your wife is fine. She's sleeping now, but you can see her during visiting hours tonight."

"But Sister, I have to be back at Alder Hey tonight. Please, can I come in now… just for a few minutes?"

"You'll get me shot," she laughed, for hospital visiting rules were strict at that time. "You can stay for five minutes, but no longer."

-0-0-0-0-0-

I took a black cab to the hospital, where I'd left my Ford Prefect. *Was it only a few hours ago I had pulled into the visitors' car park?*

Sister O'Hara was at her desk when I knocked on her open office door.

I stood on the threshold as she looked up. "Your wife is at the far end of the ward on the left-hand side," she said. "Just a few minutes, mind, and then you'll have to go."

"Thank you, Sister."

I pushed open the swing-door and my nostrils twitched at the faint scent of soiled nappies.

She was lying on her side, facing away from me, as I approached. The hunch of her shoulders confirmed her misery; the only mother without a baby. I shook her arm and she turned towards me. Her hair was tousled, damp with sweat, her eyes were red, and tiny tributaries of blood vessels were tattooed on her cheeks. Our embrace was fierce.

"Your face looks like a blood-orange, Rio," I said, poking gentle fun at the girl I adored, raising a brief smile.

"How is the baby?" she asked, huskily.

"You mean Karen?" I replied. Our baby now had a name.

"Yes. Sister O'Hara told me about the mix-up, but Karen sounds nice. What's wrong with her?"

Where was I to begin? I decided to give her the short, sanitised version I was to use on many occasions over the next few days—a quick definition of *spina bifida* and *hydrocephalus*, and the general treatment Karen would receive. I couldn't bear to tell her a valve was to be inserted into our daughter's brain, with a drain into her heart. How could I tell her Karen was almost certainly never going to walk?

Rita's face paled, and she buried her face in my chest. I stroked her hair.

"Karen is in good hands. The surgeon told me she would be fine. Apparently, they do these operations all the time. She'll be fine, you'll see."

"When is she having the operation?" Her words were muffled.

"Right about now."

"What! You mean today?" She jolted away from me but held onto my hand.

I tried to keep my voice steady. "They have to do it right away to prevent infection."

Sister O'Hara entered the ward and pointedly looked at her watch. I waved "okay" and kissed my wife. "I'll see you later, on the way back from Alder Hey. We should know more by then." She released my hand, and I walked away without a backward glance, my misery compounded by Rita's despair.

-0-0-0-0-0-

I was back outside the neo-natal unit ten minutes before the scheduled start of visiting time. A "No Admittance" sign was visible through the frosted glass door. I had telephoned before leaving, and a staff nurse had told me Karen was back from surgery, the operation had gone according to plan, and she was "as well as could be expected", which seemed like a well-rehearsed line.

After a few minutes, the shadow of a nurse appeared through the frosted glass and the "No Admittance" sign transformed itself to "Parents Only". The nurse opened the door and invited me in with a wave of her hand. I followed her down the ward until I arrived at the room where I had left Karen several hours earlier.

I looked through the window in the door. She was lying in much the same position as I had left her, except now her head was swathed in bandages, a plastic tube snaking from beneath the "turban" through a circular access port in the incubator, and into a bottle partly filled with a dark liquid, presumably blood. A further tube, with a syringe connector attached, emerged from her nose and was taped to her face. Wires ran from her chest to a bleeping heart monitor.

I opened the door and sat on one of two grey plastic chairs. She was sleeping, her chest barely moving, as she breathed the misty, highly-oxygenated air within the incubator. *This wasn't how it was supposed to be. I should have been out with my family and friends celebrating my baby daughter's birth with a few beers, not sitting in front of an incubator wondering if she was going to live or die.* Tears of self-pity pooled in my eyes.

The door opened behind me and I turned. Peter Rickman was dressed in the green gown and rubber boots of a surgeon. We shook hands and he sat next to me, leaning close. Tiny spatters of blood stained his gown. "She's a little fighter. The next few days will be critical, but the surgery to repair her back and insert the shunt valve has been successful, and all we can do now is wait. We are feeding her through a tube for the moment and treating her with antibiotics."

"I've been thinking about what you told me earlier about the valve. What will happen when she grows? Will a bigger valve be required?"

"Let me explain it again in a little more detail. We call the device a "shunt". It's effectively a tube with a one-way valve to control the rate of drainage of cerebro-spinal fluid. The valve has a pump to prevent back-flow into the brain." He held his thumb and index finger an inch or so apart. "The upper end of the tube is inserted through a small hole drilled in the skull into one of the brain's four main cavities, known as ventricles, and the lower end is fed under the skin, behind the ear, down the neck, into the chest, and into one of the chambers of the heart, where it flows back into the bloodstream." His finger traced a line from the side of his head, behind his left ear, to the front of his collar-bone.

I nodded dully, beginning to feel nauseous.

"In most cases the shunt is expected to stay in place for life, although alterations or revisions might be required from time to time. As a child grows, the tube to the heart may become too short, and an operation to lengthen it may be necessary. Also, the valve may become blocked or experience a mechanical failure and, in this case, the shunt might have to be replaced."

"How will we know if the valve becomes blocked?"

"When a shunt blockage occurs, the patient will experience severe headache, accompanied by vomiting, drowsiness, and sometimes muscular spasms and fits."

I was numb, almost too traumatised to speak. "Is there... is there any paralysis?"

"Your daughter is at least partially paralysed from the waist down, but it's too soon to know the full extent."

"And you don't know what causes *spina bifida*?"

"There are a number of theories, but research is inconclusive so far. Some researchers believe it's related to the consumption of blighted potatoes."

Potatoes? We ate potatoes almost every day! Chipped, mashed, boiled, roasted. Every meal included potatoes. My lips tightened and I shook my head, eyes bleary with the onset of tears. I shuddered, cleared my throat, regained my composure. "Are many children born with *spina bifida*?"

"Worldwide, we think around one child in 800 is born with the condition, but there seems to be a greater incidence of it in the UK, and particularly in the northwest of England."

"How many survive?"

He didn't try to dodge my question. "Your daughter has a reasonable chance of survival if she gets over the next few weeks without any setbacks. Hopefully, she will become stronger. The greatest risk is infection, so we are treating her aggressively with antibiotics to counter this threat."

"And what about the future? If she survives."

He placed his hand on mine, held it there for a moment. "She may be able to walk with the aid of leg braces, but most likely her mobility will be severely restricted, and she'll require a wheelchair."

That'll save me a few pounds in dancing lessons, I thought. My faint smile turned into a strangled leer, as I fought back the tears.

Mr Rickman stood up to leave. We shook hands, and this time I squeezed a little harder, held on a little longer. I wanted to thank him for all he had done, but it wasn't easy to express in words the huge debt of gratitude I felt for the man who was desperately trying to save my daughter's life. I hoped I would get a chance to do so later.

He squeezed my shoulder and left me alone with Karen.

-0-0-0-0-0-

Rita was sitting up in bed when I arrived at the maternity ward fifteen minutes before visiting time was over. Her face was strained, but she looked a little better, had a little more colour in her cheeks. "How is the baby?" she asked.

"She's had the surgery, and the doctor says it was successful. She was sleeping when I saw her, and they are feeding her through a tube. The next few weeks are critical, but she should recover. There's some paralysis in her legs, but it's too early to say if it'll be permanent."

"She could be paralysed?" The look of despair on Rita's face made me pause for a second.

"Yes."

"What else?"

"She's had a valve inserted in her head to drain away excess fluid on the brain, and her back has been repaired. She's very ill but, if she doesn't get any infections, she should pull through."

"When can I see her?"

"Sister O'Hara told me you'll have to stay in hospital for another day or two, and then you can go to Alder Hey to see the baby."

Rita brightened at this news, but I learned later the three days she spent in the maternity ward, looking on as beaming mothers held and fed their babies, were the worst of her life. She spent much of the time screened off from the rest of the ward, crying into her pillow.

At that moment, one of the nurses shouted down the ward, "Time visitors please!" I was relieved because I didn't want to go into any more detail.

We kissed goodbye and I left. At the end of the ward I turned and looked back. Rita was crying. I waved, smiling my reassurance, blowing a kiss. She buried her head in her pillow.

-0-0-0-0-0-

That evening, during supper at my parents' house, I went over everything again for Mum, who already knew a little from a telephone call I had made earlier, and Dad, who had now returned from a long Sunday at work. Mum hugged me and we cried together. Dad tried to comfort us, but there was no comfort to be found.

At around 11 o'clock I called the neo-natal unit. "No change", was the answer to my request for an update on my daughter's condition, which I took to be good news.

I went to bed after the most traumatic day of my young life, not knowing what the future might hold, deciding the only way to deal with this was to take one day at a time. Rita and I were young and healthy. We would cope. We'd help Karen overcome her disabilities, strive to make her life as comfortable, and normal, as possible.

I lay awake, unable to sleep because of the dark thoughts whirling around my mind.

How can there be a God? What kind of God would allow precious children to be born with such terrible disabilities? Life is hard enough without putting more obstacles in their path. What kind of God could allow this to happen to my child?

Eventually, succumbing to exhaustion, I slept and dreamt of little girls in leg irons and huge heavy shoes, like tiny deep-sea divers, dancing ponderous pirouettes.

Two

The ward sister at Alder Hey's neo-natal unit intercepted us on our way to see Karen at visiting time. This was Rita's first visit after being discharged from the maternity ward, and she had been looking forward to this moment with eager impatience. Circumstances so far had denied her the simple maternal pleasure of holding her baby.

The sister's thin face was grave, as she led us into her office. A watch was pinned to her blue uniform like a medal of honour. Rolling thunder reverberated against the window pane. "Sister," I said, "this is my wife, Rita." They shook hands.

"Pleased to meet you, Mrs. Verinder. You're both so young, aren't you?" We nodded in unison. She appeared troubled, flashes of red on her cheeks. "I'm sorry to tell you Karen's condition has deteriorated. She has severe congestion of the lungs and the doctors have diagnosed *bronchial pneumonia*."

Rita and I exchanged darting, nervous glances. "Is it serious?" I asked.

"For a new-born, it's very serious. For a new-born with Karen's conditions, bronchial pneumonia is critical."

I flinched. Rita covered her mouth with a hand. For the past few days, Karen had appeared to be getting over her surgery. The shunt valve, regulating the cerebro-spinal fluid in and around her brain, was working perfectly; she appeared to be free from infection and on the way to recovery. This setback hit us like a sudden tropical squall.

The ward sister continued, "You can see Karen now, but one of our respiratory specialists, Dr Evans, would like to talk to you. I'll let him know you're here." She picked up the black telephone receiver and dialled a number.

We traipsed out of the office and along the corridor to Karen's room. I inched open the door and peeked inside. She lay on her side in the incubator, a tiny finger looped around her nasal feeding tube. We sat, and the thunderheads rumbling menacingly overhead reflected our mood. Karen was sleeping, but her breathing was irregular, and there was a discernible blueness in her lips. The bandage on her head had been replaced by a smaller dressing, and the outline of the closely-sutured three-inch scar was clearly visible.

"Poor little mite," Rita said, reaching through a porthole to stroke Karen's hand. I stepped back, giving her a precious moment alone with our daughter. "Hello, beautiful, we're going to take good care of you, yes we are." She spoke in the quirky childish tone adults habitually use when speaking to young babies.

I bit my lower lip. *Please, God, don't take Karen from us now!* Although it was natural I would turn to God in these circumstances, my beliefs had undergone a radical change during the past few days. Now, when I exhorted God, I was appealing to destiny, not to a heavenly Father, who had burdened my baby daughter with such a heavy load.

We sat, staring into the incubator. I squeezed Rita's hand. "She'll get through this, Rio. The surgeon told me she's a fighter." Rita wiped away a tear.

The door opened and Dr Evans came in, introduced himself, and shook hands. He removed a clutter of linen and dressings from a chair in the corner, pulled the chair up close, and sat down. He had a brown mole, sprouting hairs, on his lower-left cheek.

"I understand Sister Harrison has already told you Karen has contracted pneumonia?" He spoke with a friendly Australian or New Zealand accent. My head bobbed in assent. "Pneumonia is a serious inflammation of the lungs which causes the air sacs to fill with mucus and the bloodstream to become starved of oxygen. When there is too little oxygen in the blood, the body's cells are unable to work properly, and this increases the risk of infection." He ended each sentence with a distinctive questioning tone, endemic to the Antipodes. "There are a number of different types of pneumonia, and Karen has a condition called *bacterial bronchial pneumonia*. We are treating her with strong antibiotics, but she is very seriously ill."

"What are her chances?" My voice wavered.

"It's difficult to say. Karen has a fever and our priority is to control her temperature, and to administer antibiotics to help her immune system fight the infection."

Rita cried softly beside me.

"Try not to worry," Dr Evans said unconvincingly, as he got up to leave, laying a consoling hand on Rita's shoulder. "The nursing staff are monitoring Karen closely and, for the moment, her condition is stable."

We sat in silence, except for the occasional sniff, watching Karen's chest rise and fall, until a nurse informed us visiting time was over.

-0-0-0-0-0-

Later that night we ate dinner at our terraced house in Walton, a northern suburb of Liverpool. The house had been dilapidated when we bought it, but much of the renovation work was complete in anticipation of Karen's birth. Rita had helped with the painting and decorating, even when heavily pregnant. We sat at a polished drop-leaf table, eating baked beans on toast. Karen's shining Pedigree pram stood in a corner in its original cellophane wrapping.

"She's in the best possible place for treatment," I said. "The neo-natal unit is one of the best in the world."

"I suppose so." Rita's tone was desultory.

"They treated her with antibiotics immediately after they diagnosed pneumonia, so that's in our favour, too."

"Yes." She moved beans around her plate with a fork. Neither of us had much of an appetite. Rita stood and took her plate to the kitchen. I heard her scrape her dinner into the bin, fill the kettle with water from the brass cold-water tap, and light a gas jet on the cooker. If we needed hot water for tea, coffee or washing, we had to boil it. The house didn't have a bathroom; we had a draughty brick privy at the bottom of the yard, but the new bathroom I was planning remained on the drawing board due to lack of funds.

We drank tea and watched television, both of us thinking only of our baby fighting for life in a hospital incubator. Rita decided on an early night. I remained deep in thought, wondering what lay ahead.

Would she... could she... survive the pneumonia virus when she was not yet four days old? Would I ever hold my baby again, enjoy that unique new-born odour you could almost taste?

I fell asleep in my lumpy armchair. I had no answers. The high-pitched tone, signalling the end of television transmissions for the night, jolted me awake. I switched off the old black-and-white set and the incandescent dot in the centre of the screen burst and died.

Many of my hopes and dreams for the future had been wrecked on the rocks of a new reality during the past few days. I had never been so dejected in my entire life. I had to snap out of it, become more upbeat. If

Karen recovered… *when* she recovered… we had to ensure she lived as rich a life as possible.

-0-0-0-0-0-

The next morning, after a restless night, I called the neo-natal unit from a pay phone on City Road. A nurse reported a slight improvement and, by the time we arrived for the evening visit, Karen was much better.

Over the next few days, the blueness in her lips became a healthy pink, and she gained a few ounces. She was awake more, the operation wounds on her head and lower back were healing, and there were no further complications. Occasionally, she was allowed to lie on her back and, at such times, she would instinctively wave her arms about. From her legs, however, there was no movement whatsoever, not even a twitch.

A week after the pneumonia infection had been vanquished, we received some good news. Although the surgeons had previously expressed concern over the function of Karen's bowel and bladder, both appeared to be working normally. For the moment, she would require no further treatment.

Our optimism was short-lived. The pneumonia returned with deadly intent, and Sister Harrison warned us Karen would probably not survive this relapse. We were now permitted to stay in the unit for as long as we wished. Karen was categorised as *on the danger list*. We maintained a constant vigil throughout that day, only leaving for toilet breaks. Our baby girl was wracked by coughing spells, which weakened her pitiful cries.

I looked out the window towards Springfield Park and the storm clouds had returned.

Presently, a nurse knocked and entered. In her gossamer-gloved hand, she carried a small kidney-shaped bowl containing a phial and a plastic syringe. Pressing the needle through a rubber seal in the phial, she withdrew a precise quantity of liquid into the syringe. Moving to the back of the incubator, she inserted her hands through the portholes, pushed the syringe into a connector attached to Karen's tiny wrist, and forced the aggressive antibiotic fluid into Karen's bloodstream.

This procedure was repeated every two hours, but Karen's coughing became progressively worse, and her lips and fingernails remained blue. Later that evening, though, I thought I could detect a slight improvement in her breathing.

Close to midnight, a nurse checked Karen's temperature.

She smiled. "Her temperature's gone down. The fever seems to have broken."

I squeezed Rita's hand and looked up to the heavens. "Thank God for that."

"Why don't you go home for some rest and come back in the morning," the nurse suggested.

We took her advice. Collapsing into bed with exhaustion, my sleep was disturbed by another vivid dream. Karen was a little girl around five years old. She was wearing a pink tulle bridesmaid's dress and was running toward me, arms outstretched. I ran towards her, she ran towards me, but the distance between us remained unchanged.

Back at the neo-natal unit at eight the next morning, the blue tint in Karen's lips and fingernails had faded. She still coughed occasionally, but the improvement in just 24 hours was incredible. We spent a long day beside the incubator, occasionally inserting a finger into one of her clenched fists to let her know we were there.

Another week passed, and each day Karen became a little stronger. Her tube-fed milk had been thickened with a little rice cereal, and she seemed to digest this mixture better. Previously, she had regurgitated some of her milk due to a condition known as *reflux*, which had hampered her development. Her wounds healed and her hair began to grow back, although the scar on her head had an ugly bump where the valve was positioned. Karen's name was removed from the danger list and we resumed conventional visiting—seven o'clock to eight o'clock each evening.

-0-0-0-0-0-

One evening towards the end of May, having recently returned from my work as a Computer Operator, I was disturbed while scanning the headlines in the *Liverpool Echo* by a loud hammering on the door. I turned the latch, opened the door, and found a police constable standing on the quarry-tiled step.

"Mr Verinder?"

I nodded, filled with foreboding.

"We have had a message from Alder Hey. They want you there as soon as possible."

"W… what's wrong?" The knot in my stomach was back.

"They didn't say. Would you like me to take you?"

"No, no. Thanks. I have my own car." I felt myself breathing quickly, as if in panic. "Thanks," I repeated, "I have my own car." I must have sounded foolish. I didn't care.

The policeman left, and I went back inside to deliver the bad news to Rita, who was cooking dinner. She quickly turned off the gas jets. My Ford Prefect, which often refused to start without a push, whirred into life at the first attempt.

We arrived at the neo-natal unit a little after 6 o'clock, delayed by the early evening homeward traffic on the busy Queens Drive ring road. Except for the occasional expletive, followed by an obscene gesture, I hardly spoke a word during the entire journey. Sister Harrison ushered us into her office and motioned us to sit down.

"I'm sorry to tell you…"

"No, please God, no," Rita whispered.

"Karen has pneumonia again," she continued. "The doctor thinks she is unlikely to survive the night. I'm so sorry." She held Rita's hand. On the drive to the hospital we had feared the worst, and now it seemed that dreaded time was almost upon us.

Sister Harrison led us to Karen's room. "Karen was doing so well," she said. "We are treating her with antibiotics, but she's not keeping her food down, and it's just a matter of time now. You can sit with her until…"

She left us alone with our grief. Our baby daughter was going to die.

Half an hour passed. We monitored the rise and fall of her shallow breathing and we waited. An hour passed. A nurse came in to administer more antibiotics and we continued our vigil. Karen convulsed and we thought we were losing her, but the rhythm of her breathing resumed. I prayed silently and, through will-power alone, tried to pass some of my strength to my baby daughter. Every hour seemed like a day.

Visitors to the unit arrived and left. I looked up at the clock on the wall; it was nine o'clock. The next dose of powerful antibiotic fluid was injected into her bloodstream. We continued to watch Karen's every breath. I couldn't bring myself to look at the heart monitor but was aware of its continuous bleeping in the background. I waited for the long uninterrupted tone that would follow the final heartbeat, but it continued to pulse.

Rita and I were reluctant to leave Karen's side for even a minute. The clock showed half-past eleven and we took turns to use the toilet. Nurses came to check on Karen and went away again. The fever raged on.

I fell asleep sitting in the hard, plastic chair. Suddenly I was awakened by a sharp clunk, but it was only a nurse closing the door after checking on Karen. Rita, too, had drifted into a shallow sleep, but she woke when I stirred. Karen was still breathing and the hands of the clock had inched forward to a little after half-past one. The heart monitor continued its hypnotic rhythm.

A young nurse brought in cups of sweet tea. Karen coughed. We peered through the misty atmosphere of the incubator, and she settled again.

We sat beside the incubator through the remainder of that interminable night. Sister Harrison, back on duty at seven, was surprised Karen was still clinging to life, albeit by a slender thread. Gradually the crisis ended. The worst of the fever had abated, and, although Karen's lungs were still congested, the pneumonia bacteria appeared to have been conquered for the third and, we hoped, final time.

Over the next few weeks, Karen made a full recovery from the insidious pneumonia, and our next objective was to wean her off tube feeding. Sister Harrison had told us, during the first weeks of life, the reflex suck-and-swallow action of a baby is instinctive, and a new-born will quickly learn to trust the feeding process. However, when a baby has been tube-fed for several weeks, as Karen had, this trust had to be nurtured.

Karen was now allowed out of the incubator for periods during the day so that Rita could feed her milk from a bottle to supplement the tube feed. At first, due to a lack of oral stimulation and experience of swallowing,

Karen refused to suck on the teat, but with a great deal of patience on Rita's part, she gradually accepted increasing quantities of milk from a bottle.

Her reliance on the feeding tube became the biggest obstacle to Karen being discharged from hospital, and this acted as an incentive for Rita to wean her off the tube feed as soon as possible. After more than six weeks in the neo-natal unit, the feeding tube was removed and Karen began to feed only from the bottle. She was underweight and her health was still fragile, but her condition improved every day.

During the time Karen was in Alder Hey, Rita and I had witnessed the desolate grief of a number of parents whose babies were taken from them. We had been spared this terrible ordeal, but we had been close to the edge, and the experience was not one we cared to repeat. For the time being, however, our anguish was over.

-0-0-0-0-0-

Waves of wispy blue smoke rolled under the low ceiling, and the sweet, woody smell of Golden Virginia permeated the air. A buxom singer, bleached blonde, thirty-something, tight spangled dress struggling to constrain the rolls of flesh beneath, belted out a Connie Francis number from a small stage at the front of the crowded concert room. She was backed by an organist and a drummer, both of whom belied their advanced years with energetic performances. Quite a change from the pulsating 60's sounds of the *Cavern* and *Iron Door* clubs that Rita and I had frequented just a few short months earlier, but fun nonetheless.

The lyrics were familiar.

You were only foolin', while I was fallin' in love…

Mum sang along in her off-key voice over the babble of background noise. She fancied herself as a sultry Marlene Dietrich sound-alike, but her party-piece rendition of *Give Me a Nail and a Hammer and a Picture to Hang on the Wall* didn't quite live up to her billing.

It's a story as old as Adam and Eve, I was makin' love but you were makin' believe…

Two days earlier, I had celebrated my twenty-first birthday by feeding my baby daughter in the neo-natal unit of Liverpool's Alder Hey Children's Hospital. Another week and she would be home. This was the first time my wife, Rita, and I had been out together since Karen's birth. Now, I was surrounded by family and friends and getting merrily drunk.

You lied to me with kisses, that I was once dreamin' of…

I winked at Mum as she sang, and she beamed that special smile she reserved only for me. A mother's love is a truly wondrous gift, I thought, as the copious draughts of Younger's Tartan Bitter infused me with large doses of sentimentality.

You were only foolin' dear, while I was fallin' in love.

The audience clapped and cheered, and Dad jumped up from his seat and took the microphone from the perspiring singer. Dad was the club's Concert Secretary. "Ladies and gentleman, let's hear it once more for Pauline Danson..." Random isolated whistles punctuated the overly zealous applause. Dad waited for the hubbub to subside and for the chubby Miss Danson to wobble off the stage. "Pauline will be back after the Bingo for the second half of our show. In the meantime, I'll leave you with the sounds of Bob and Len." Dad, compere for the evening, replaced the microphone in its stand and re-joined our group. The organist played the opening bars of *Mac the Knife,* and the drummer swished a catchy rhythm with wire brushes on a snare drum and cymbals.

I had hoped my baby daughter, Karen, would be home for my twenty-first birthday on July 7, but this was not to be. No matter; only another week and she would be out of hospital. For the first time in two months I felt relaxed.

Suddenly, a female arm snaked around my neck and a wet kiss slurped in my ear. "Davie, sweetheart. Happy birthday, darlin'." Ada O'Carroll, a petite, curvaceous blonde and a friend of Mum's, teetered on her trademark six-inch stiletto heels, which doubled as vicious weapons in the drunken bar fights she was inclined to instigate at the slightest flutter of an unwelcome hand on her ample posterior. I once saw her split an unfortunate admirer's scalp like an over-ripe plum with a single fluent, practiced move that would have graced a Bruce Lee movie. Tonight, though, Ada was maudlin and touchy-feely. "How's the baby?" she whispered in my ear while running her fingers lightly but expertly along the small of my back. Ada was a natural flirt. She also had a well-honed predilection for younger men, which evidently did not exclude her best friend's son.

"She's coming home soon, Ada," I managed through constricted vocal cords. "The doctors are really pleased with her."

"That's good, darlin". You take care now." Ada's lingering fingers said a long goodbye to my spine and she tottered off towards the bar.

The conversation in our party was understandably dominated by the circumstances of Karen's birth and subsequent treatment. I was chatting to Dad's brother, my Uncle Ted, describing the long night Rita and I had spent with Karen during an almost fatal third bout of pneumonia. My eyes were a little misty.

Uncle Ted looked at me with tenderness and concern in equal measures. He had long been a favourite uncle, offering a kind and sympathetic shoulder whenever it was needed, together with copious helpings of pea soup for which he was famous. He slipped his arm around my shoulders and squeezed. He looked troubled. "Dave," he ventured, "maybe it would have been better—for you and Rita—if Karen hadn't survived. You're young enough to…"

What? I must have misheard him. Surely, he wasn't suggesting that my darling daughter would've been better off dead?

I knocked his arm away and stood up, anger bubbling up inside me like a hot geyser. "What the hell are you talking about?" I spluttered. The conversation in our group hushed. Mum looked at Dad. Dad looked at me. Rita looked aghast. "How can you say such a thing?" I yelled.

Uncle Ted recoiled as if I'd punched him and spread his hands in a calming gesture. I pushed him away and stalked from the room and out of the club.

In the cool evening air, my anger simmered as I paced the pavement. How dare he suggest Karen would be better off dead! She'd been fighting for her life the past two months, had come through unimaginable ordeals, and he says we'd be better off without her! Didn't he know how much we loved her, how much of a bond had been forged between us?

"Dave, wait!" Dad had followed me down the street. He caught up, held me tight, tried to calm me down, tried to explain what his elder brother had meant. "Listen, son. Ted was only thinking of your welfare. You and Rita are both young. You can have more children. He knows how difficult it will be for you in the future, what a burden it will be."

So that was the official family line! We were young and could have more children! I shrugged Dad away. "I don't want another baby. I want the one I already have!"

He grabbed me, held me in a bear-hug, while hot, bitter tears streamed down my face. After a few minutes, we walked across the road to the Derby Arms. A double vodka and tonic helped me regain my composure.

"I can't believe anyone could think we'd be better off without Karen."

"I know, son. It was the wrong thing to say, the wrong time to say it, but Ted meant only the best for you. He loves you; he didn't mean to hurt you."

Several drinks later, we re-joined the party. Uncle Ted and I shook hands and hugged. Harmony was restored. Rita and Mum looked at me questioningly. I smiled.

Uncle Ted had done me a huge favour. Without realising it, he had instilled in me a steely determination. Not only would Karen live, she would live as full a life as it was possible to lead. No obstacle would stand in our way. No mountain, no river, no institution, no medical problem. Nothing.

-0-0-0-0-0-

Karen continued to keep her food down and gained weight. The muscles that compressed her bowel and bladder were below normal strength, but both functions were working and were of no great concern to the doctors. The nurses showed us how to gently massage Karen's lower bowel to encourage its normal operation, and this became a regular task.

We were also taught how to be sure her shunt valve was working properly. Positioned just behind Karen's right ear, under the skin, the flexible non-return valve, which let fluid out but prevented it from flowing back, could be gently pressed. If it sprang back to its normal position immediately, then we knew the valve was working as it should. If it stayed depressed or was slow to return to its normal position, then there was probably a blockage. It became routine, whenever Karen was cranky, to check her valve.

Rita was now allowed to be with Karen throughout the day, feeding, nursing and changing her, and generally getting to know her. Making up for lost time, mother and daughter thrived. It was such a pleasure to see Rita so happy, and our daughter so well, after all we had been through. We longed for the day when we could take our baby home.

In the next room to Karen, lying in a similar incubator, was another baby suffering from *spina bifida* and *hydrocephalus*. We learned her name was Susan, the daughter of Peter and Margaret Jervis, and she had been born almost three weeks after Karen.

We now knew people with similar problems, and this helped us feel less isolated; gradually we came to terms with our predicament. Under Rita's watchful eye, Karen continued to improve and, one extra special Thursday night when I arrived at the hospital from work, Sister Harrison delivered the good news.

Tomorrow, Karen could come home!

Three

On Friday, July 15, 1966, Karen was finally discharged from Alder Hey. For the first time, she wore regular baby clothes, and she slept in a slatted wooden crib next to our bed. During the first week, we fretted over every sound and movement, but we eventually settled into a routine of bottle feeding, changing nappies, daily baths, and other regular baby chores.

Two weeks after Karen came home—the Saturday of England's first soccer World Cup Final—I helped Rita bathe and dress our daughter. After washing Karen in her plastic bath, using a soft sponge and Johnson's baby soap, I laid her on her back atop a fluffy, white bath towel. I wrapped the towel around her and picked her up. Sitting on our second-hand tweed settee in the lounge, I gently rubbed her dry.

Children's Favourites, a radio programme hosted by Uncle Mac—Derek McCulloch—was playing *Gilly Gilly Ossenfeffer Katzenellen Bogen by the Sea*. I sang along to the chorus with Max Bygraves, as I tickled Karen's tummy. I was rewarded with her first smile.

Rita laid out Karen's clothes, a pink satin dress with ruffled lace around the neck and cuffs, and matching bootees. I draped Karen over my left arm and sprinkled talcum powder on her back and bottom. Her lower back was a mass of puckered scar tissue. Three distinct suture lines ran at wide angles towards a central point where the spinal cord had been exposed at birth.

With moist eyes, I kissed the top of Karen's head. Her hair was soft on my lips, like strands of pure Italian silk. Rita massaged Karen's feet as I pulled a tiny cotton vest over her head and arms, covering the scars. After putting on her dress and bootees, Karen now looked like any other ten-week-old baby girl.

Rita decided to take Karen with her on a shopping trip while I watched the World Cup Final on television. After Rita had settled Karen into her pram, I manoeuvred it out of the hall, down the front step, and onto the pavement, before applying the brake. Mum's younger sister, my Auntie Eileen, lived a few doors away with her husband, Norman, and my three young cousins, Norman Junior, Eddie and Sheila. Uncle Norman's lorry was parked outside his house and, with the tailgate lowered, he reached inside towards a stack of cardboard cartons.

"Nice afternoon, Uncle Norm," I said. He turned around, laden with boxes. Placing the cartons on the pavement, he rubbed the base of his spine and let rip with a prodigious fart. If farting was an Olympic sport, Uncle Norm would win gold every time. I loved the guy but he had the manners of a rutting warthog in the mating season. Also, I've never forgiven him for dressing me in a blue silk knickerbocker suit when I was a four-year-old pageboy at his wedding.

"Yeah," he wheezed. "How's the baby?"

Before, I could answer, our immediate neighbour, Mrs. Hughes, whose house was a mirror image of ours with only a thin brick dividing wall between us, opened her front door. "Cooeee, Davie," Mrs. Hughes said. "How's the little one?" She hobbled out, legs creaking, and peeked into the pram. Her grey hair straggled around her wrinkled face like thick strands of coarse string and her clothes smelled musty. Uncle Norman disappeared inside his house.

Mrs. Hughes had lost her husband several years earlier and lived alone. She was a little eccentric, I thought, although most of the other neighbours thought her a raving lunatic. Late at night, she was apt to scream obscenities at the devil who, she claimed, sat on her shoulder every evening after dark.

"She's coming along well, thanks, Mrs. Hughes."

Rita appeared behind me and grimaced as she saw the old lady lean into the pram. She grabbed the handle and kicked off the brake. Mrs. Hughes stepped back.

"I won't be too long, Dave," Rita said, as she set off towards the shopping centre in County Road.

Mrs. Hughes grabbed my arm with gnarled fingers. "Davie, will you do me a favour?"

"Of course, Mrs. Hughes."

"A light bulb in my bedroom needs to be replaced, and I can't reach it."

"No problem."

I followed Mrs. Hughes into her house and up the stairs. A black cat perched on the banister, its spine arched and its hackles up. I inched past, back to the wall, as the cat's feral eyes monitored my progress. The heavy curtains in the bedroom were closed. In the gloom, I could see a chair had been placed immediately underneath a bare light bulb hanging from the ceiling. I stood on the chair and reached up to remove the burnt-out bulb from its socket.

Mrs. Hughes suddenly circled my legs with surprisingly strong arms and buried her face in my groin. I dropped the bulb and it shattered on the bare floorboards. "I won't let you fall, Davie," she said, as her mouth moved against my private parts and her hands snaked up the back of my thighs.

Shit! The old goat has me by the balls! My voice was a strangled falsetto. "I'm fine Mrs. Hughes. Will you please stop that!"

"I really miss my Albert, you know, Davie."

I pried her rheumatic fingers from my backside, and with two hands on top of her head, shoved her away. As she staggered back, I grabbed the new light bulb out of her outstretched hand, screwed it in before she could regain her balance, and backed out of the room. With a screech, the cat pounced, and sank its claws into my back. I yelped, reached behind me, grabbed it by the scruff of the neck, and flung it to the floor.

I sprinted down the stairs, through the open door and into the street. I heard Mrs. Hughes coming after me. "Davie, cooeee, Davie, where are you?"

I fled into the sanctuary of my own home, slammed the door shut, and leaned against it for a moment. Seconds later, the laughter started as a low rumble deep in my throat and ended in a fit of stomach-aching, tear-streaming, thigh-slapping hilarity.

That night, while Rita and I celebrated England's World Cup victory against West Germany with several Watney's pale ales, Mrs. Hughes ranted at the devil with increased ferocity.

-0-0-0-0-0-

I returned home from work one evening when Rita was about to bathe Karen. I offered to undress our three-month-old baby while Rita ran some warm water into a duck-shaped plastic bath. I sat on the settee and lay Karen down on her back across my lap. She had recently been fed and she cooed softly, following my movements with her eyes.

I took off her Crimplene romper suit, unpinned her nappy, and left it draped over my knees. I then expressed her bowel by gently pressing on her lower abdomen, singing as I massaged.

The wheels on the bus go round and round,
Round and round, round and round,
The wheels on the bus go round and round,

Squish, squish, squish.

I squeezed her tummy with each *squish*. Suddenly, there was a whoosh of air, and yellow baby poo spurted over the carpet. Rita came in from the kitchen with the bath, convulsed with laughter, and spilled the soapy water over our newly-laid carpet. Karen blew spit bubbles.

The next day, though, Karen was a little cranky, and Rita noticed fluid, presumably cerebro-spinal fluid, leaking out of the operation scar on her lower back. Rita tested Karen's valve, feeling for the rubber seal under the skin behind her ear and pressing it. The valve appeared to be working. However, we had been warned leaking fluid could be a sign of abnormally high pressure in the cranial cavity.

We rushed Karen to the Casualty Unit at Alder Hey, where she was immediately taken to the Radiology Department to undergo a procedure known as a *myelogram*, which involves the injection of a barium dye into the spinal canal to make the canal more clearly visible on x-rays.

As the radiologist pushed the needle into Karen's back, she screamed and her face contorted. I looked on, feeling helpless, and held her hand, my body protected from the x-rays by a lead-lined apron. Hot tears coursed down my cheeks. Rita stood out of sight behind a protective screen.

The first attempt to push the needle through Karen's lower vertebrae met with dogged resistance, and the radiologist withdrew. Feeling with his latex-gloved fingers for another likely spot, seemingly impervious to

Karen's screams of pain, he tried again, without success. On the third attempt, the needle pierced the bony barrier and he injected the silver liquid.

A tearful Rita was ushered away by a nurse.

After the x-ray was taken, I wrapped Karen in a shawl and cuddled her until her cries settled into an occasional quivering sigh. I then took her outside into the corridor where Rita was being consoled by the nurse.

"Is she okay?" Rita sobbed, as I handed Karen to her. I nodded and wiped away a stray tear from my cheek. We walked back to Casualty and awaited the results.

The x-ray confirmed the build-up of pressure, and the neurosurgeons decided Karen's shunt valve was faulty and had to be replaced. Rita and I fretted in the waiting room during the operation, hardly a word passing between us.

When Karen was wheeled back into the unit in an incubator, it was a case of *déjà vu*. Once again, bandages enshrouded our baby daughter's head. A snaking drain tube dripped dark blood into a bottle, a feeding tube dangled from her nose, and an intravenous connector encircled her wrist. A heart monitor emitted sinister bleeping sounds.

One step forward and two steps back.

Karen spent the next seven days in the neo-natal unit. We visited her each day and, after she had recovered from the trauma of the surgery, the dark veil of misery gradually lifted. Karen's recuperation was swift, and after a few days, she was disconnected from the heart monitor, the drain and feeding tubes were removed, and we were allowed to take her out of the incubator to feed her.

Gazing down at my darling daughter as she sucked greedily on the teat of her bottle, I marvelled at the capacity of the human body to recover from affliction. If she could survive the trials and tribulations of the past few months, surely, she could survive anything?

Karen was discharged from hospital on the morning of Saturday, July 30, and made a complete recovery from the valve replacement surgery. She quickly settled back into a regular feeding and sleeping routine.

Several times each day, Rita massaged Karen's legs and feet. Occasionally, one of her legs twitched involuntarily, but otherwise, they displayed no signs of movement.

During the summer months, Rita would take Karen to nearby Stanley Park in her pram, lay a tartan shawl on the edge of the duck pond and snuggle Karen down beside her. She would tell me about these excursions when I came home from my job as a Computer Operator with English Electric. Gradually, the omnipresent edge of concern dissipated and we started to feel like a normal family.

-0-0-0-0-0-

In September, when Karen was four months old, we kept an appointment with an orthopaedic specialist at Whiston Hospital. Eric Strach, Consultant Orthopaedic Surgeon at Whiston, was passionate in his belief that a child born with *spina bifida* should learn to walk with the aid of a suitable support mechanism. Regular leg braces, such as those worn by a polio sufferer, for example, were not suitable because the muscles in the hips, buttocks, and lower back were not usually strong enough. Mr Strach solved this problem by adding a body brace to the leg support structure.

He swore by the psychological benefits of standing and walking. The resultant sense of achievement, Mr Strach reasoned, created a positive outlook for both the child and the parents. He offered us hope for the future.

Mr Strach studied the x-rays of Karen's lower body with the aid of a light box positioned on the wall of his office. "Look here," he said in his endearing Czechoslovakian accent, as he pointed to each of her hips in turn. "Both Karen's hips are subluxated, which means they are approximately half-way between dislocated and normal. This is quite common in a *spina bifida* patient due to an imbalance of muscles around the hips. We need to fit her with a special splint, which will force the hips into the correct position."

"How long will she need the splint?" I asked.

"For about three months. The splint will create some handling difficulties for you, but the awkwardness will be worth it because we'll be able to fit her with callipers at the age she would normally be walking. If her hips are not positioned correctly, putting her into callipers would not be possible."

Mr Strach led us into a treatment room and asked me to lay Karen down on a couch. He then asked Rita to remove the baby's clothes. The surgeon pulled Karen's tiny legs apart, gently pushing each hip into its socket. He then placed a bow-shaped splint on top of her legs and abdomen and fastened it in place with a bandage wound around each leg.

Rita was able to put a nappy on our daughter by using a safety pin on each side, but we couldn't get the legs of Karen's romper suit over the splint, so they had to remain dangling. I lifted Karen off the treatment couch and wrapped a shawl around her legs. We made another appointment to see Mr Strach in three months' time and left for home.

Mr Strach's reference to "handling difficulties" was a supreme understatement. Karen was unable to sit up and feeding her was a job for two. With Karen facing away from me, I had to hold her upright resting the crossbar of the splint across my knees, while Rita held the bottle to her lips.

Bathing Karen was even more difficult, as we had to avoid getting the bandages wet. Karen loved the sensation of water running over her and we were loath to deprive her of this pleasure. So, with arms outstretched, I would hold Karen over the bath while Rita poured water over her with a jug. It was worth the aching arms to see her chortle with delight.

-0-0-0-0-0-

In December, we reported back to Whiston, and Mr Strach removed the splint. He instructed Rita to use double nappies for the next couple of months to keep Karen's legs slightly apart, which would increase the chances of her hips remaining in position as she grew.

A few months later, our growing nine-month-old daughter loved to sit in her play-pen surrounded by building blocks, soft fabric dolls, and alphabet picture books with thick cardboard pages. She also crawled or, more accurately, she used her forearms to drag herself around.

We had purchased a baby bouncer, a canvas bucket-seat with a strong elastic cord, which attached to the top of an open doorway. Karen loved to sit in it with her feet touching the floor. We jerked the cord so she could "feel" her feet as she bounced around. We hoped this routine would strengthen her legs.

As we started to potty-train her, we were thrilled to learn she could control her bladder and bowel functions without the need for manual expression. It would be some time before we could dispense with nappies, but whenever I sat her on her little yellow potty, before her bedtime story, and mimed a strained bearing down with a comical scrunched-up face, Karen would giggle and poo at the same time.

Reading a copy of *Link* magazine from the Association for Spina Bifida and Hydrocephalus, I noticed an advertisement for a child's trolley with a padded seat and back support. Dubbed the SHASBAH trolley, it had a ball-castor mounted on the front and two small wheels fixed to an axle at the back. It was like a de-luxe soap box cart and could be propelled by turning the rubber-clad wheels. By turning the right wheel alone, the child could turn the trolley to the left, and by turning the left wheel alone could turn it to the right. Simple yet brilliant! The trolleys were hand-made in a factory in East Kilbride, Scotland, and I immediately placed our order.

The trolley was delivered a couple of days before Karen's first birthday, and it turned out to be the best present we could have given her. Rita and I looked on with delight as, sitting on the floor, Karen ripped open the gift-wrap and tried to climb aboard. I lifted her into the seat and placed her hands on the wheels. With my hands on top of hers, I showed her how to push it along. She understood intuitively.

As we watched our little girl meander around the lounge, gurgling with pleasure, it was as though we were seeing her take her first steps. This simple trolley would allow Karen to take part in activities otherwise denied her, and the thought was as gratifying to me as the sight of a life raft to a drowning man.

-0-0-0-0-0-

One Saturday morning, soon after Karen's first birthday, Rita and I were shopping in County Road. I pushed Karen in her pram, as she cuddled her one-eyed, red-and-white Teddy Bear, which accompanied her everywhere.

Presently, we came to a pet shop. A fluffy white kitten played in the window with a screwed-up ball of paper.

"Dave, look at the little kitten. Isn't he gorgeous? Look at the little kitty, Karen." Rita was captivated. We had been thinking of acquiring a family pet, but I had in mind a goldfish or budgie. I wasn't a cat person, as Mrs. Hughes's mangy moggy had confirmed.

"Why not a hamster?" I ventured.

"Ah, look at him playing with the ball. Look, Karen."

"How about a guinea pig?" I tried again.

"We could call him, Snowy, Karen." Rita drummed her fingers on the window, and the kitten tried to lick her hand through the glass.

I gave up. Rita waited outside with Karen. A bell tinkled as I pushed the shop door open and stepped inside. A variety of birds—budgerigars, canaries, parakeets, mynahs, and others I didn't recognise—warbled and trilled. Whimpering pups added to the cacophony. On the counter, in a chrome wire cage, a blue budgerigar preened himself in a mirror. The shop smelled of pet food and animal droppings.

"Can I help you, sir?" offered a small man in a brown overall.

"How much is that doggie—I mean kitten—in the window?"

He smiled as though he'd heard the line for the first time. "One pound, nineteen shillings and sixpence, sir, including a wicker basket. A lovely choice, if you don't mind me saying."

"And what about the budgie and cage on the counter?"

"A prime specimen, sir. You have good taste, if I may say so. With the cage, that's another one pound, eight shillings and sixpence. If you buy the cat and the budgie together, I'll throw in three tins of Kit-e-Kat and a packet of Trill. You won't find a better deal than that, sir, not in the whole of Liverpool."

I thought for a second. I wanted a budgie; Rita wanted a cat. Oh, what the hell...

"I'll take them both." I extracted three pound notes and a single ten-shilling note from my wallet, handed them over, and received a silver florin in change.

The shopkeeper wrapped a large sheet of brown paper around the cage, lifted the kitten out of the window, and set it down on a mattress of shredded newspaper in a wicker basket on the counter. I took the basket outside and positioned it on the pram so Karen could see the kitten. I went back inside for the cage, and the budgie warbled a constant melody as we headed for home.

As Rita had suggested, we called the kitten Snowy, and I named the budgie Billy after Billy Liddell, the famous Liverpool footballer. Karen loved to play with the kitten. Sitting on the carpet she would dangle a ball of wool on a string and Snowy would leap for it, dragging it out of her hand, and chasing it around the floor.

One day, the kitten jumped for the ball of wool, landed on Karen's legs, and steadied himself with his claws. Karen cried out and dropped the ball as Snowy leapt off her legs, leaving oozing scratch marks in his wake. Rita and I looked at each other, eyes wide, lips forming perfect circles.

Karen could feel pain in her legs!

If she could feel pain, surely all of the neural pathways to her legs couldn't be blocked? This realisation started a chain reaction of positive thoughts in my mind... *Pain equals feeling; feeling equals control; control equals muscles; muscles equals strength...*

Later that day, as Karen sat in her high-chair, Rita helped spoon Heinz baby food into her mouth. Hidden by the tray attached to the front of the chair, I pricked Karen's legs in various places with a safety pin. Several times she jolted and her legs twitched.

Now, there was absolutely no doubt—she definitely had some feeling in her legs.

Four

I n the autumn of 1967, when Karen was sixteen months old, we travelled to Whiston Hospital in our new family car, a 1956 Morris Minor saloon, which I had bought for seventy-five pounds from a fastidious lady driver who had owned it from new. We had an appointment with Mr Strach, who was to fit Karen with her first walking aid. Four weeks earlier, we had been instructed to attend a surgical workshop and a technician had carefully measured Karen's legs and torso.

On the way to Whiston, passing through the leafy suburbs of Huyton and Prescot, Karen was strapped into her baby seat in the back, absorbed with her animal picture book. Rita sat in the front passenger seat and turned to look at Karen. "What does the doggy say?" Rita asked.

"Woof, woof!"

"And what does Snowy the kitten say?"

"Meeow, meeow!"

"And what about Billy the Budgie? What does he say?"

"Tweet, tweet!"

"And what does the little piggy say?"

"Mooo, mooo!"

"No, that's not right, silly sausage… the cow says mooo! The little piggy says oink, oink, oink!"

"Oink, oink, oink!"

As we reached the hospital, I indicated a right turn, and the orange semaphore indicator arm duly sprang out from the side of the car. Through a gap in the heavy oncoming traffic, I turned into Green Dragon Lane and glided into the visitors' car park on the left-hand side, opposite the *Green Dragon* pub.

I retrieved Karen's fold-down pushchair from the boot, while Rita unbuckled her and lifted her out of the car. Sitting in her pushchair with her picture book, Karen could have been a model in a baby food advert. Her soft strawberry-blonde hair curled precociously over her forehead, her cheeks were a plump rosy pink, and her smile was cherubic.

We reached the children's orthopaedic clinic and, after a short wait, we were called in to Mr Strach's office. I left the pushchair in the waiting room and carried Karen in.

Karen's walking aid was laid out on a treatment couch. The device consisted of strips of thin steel, designed to run down the inner and outer legs. Leather supports and straps were provided to secure the metal struts at the ankles, knees, and thighs. The leg braces were welded to a padded body support, which had a wide Velcro chest strap. The apparatus, which Mr Strach referred to as *callipers*, had lockable hinges at the hips and knees to allow the patient to sit without removing the device.

It looked like... hmmm... *What did it look like?* I wondered. A chastity belt, designed by King Arthur for his cheating Guinevere? A harness for a miniature Boadicean warhorse? Perhaps, a truss from a dungeon in the Marquis de Sade's castle?

"Hello, Karen, how are you? *Ach jo!* You look good! Hello, Mum and Dad. Please... sit... sit." Mr Strach exuded his usual ebullient charm. "Today, we will try Karen's callipers. Soon, she will walk." Mr Strach's desktop was bare, except for a manilla folder containing Karen's case notes and a silver frame containing a photograph of a handsome couple on their wedding day.

Karen sat on my knee, and Mr Strach, kneeling on the floor, laced a tiny hand-made boot onto each of Karen's feet. Each boot had holes drilled in the heels to accommodate a leg brace. He then lifted Karen on to a treatment couch and, laying her down on top of the callipers, showed us how to fit them.

First, he inserted the leg braces into the heels of the boots and secured them around Karen's ankles with leather straps. Next, he fastened each of the knee supports around the braces and wrapped wide leather straps around the top of each thigh. Finally, he secured the body brace with the Velcro strap. Karen's lower body was now encased in a steel and leather harness. Mr Strach helped me to lift her onto her feet.

"*Hej rup!* Up we go Karen!" Mr Strach said.

I stood her on the treatment couch and she clung to me. "Dadaa, dadaa!" she cried. She flung her dimpled arms around my neck.

"Shush now, baby," I soothed. "Daddy's holding you. Daddy won't let you fall... shush now, sweetheart."

Mr Strach stepped out of his office for a moment.

"How the hell is she supposed to walk trussed up like a turkey?" Rita whispered.

"I don't know, love. Let's see how she..."

Mr Strach returned with a chrome, Zimmer-style walking frame with rubber wheels on the front. Directed by Mr Strach, I placed Karen on the floor between the arms of the frame, but she continued to cling to me.

"Don't worry," Mr Strach said. "She'll gradually gain confidence. The objective is to get her used to being on her feet holding onto the walking frame. Get her accustomed to standing for longer and longer periods. Let her watch TV while standing with the frame. Or prop her up against an armchair and let her play with some toys."

A vivid image of Karen standing against a chair playing with her plastic tea set popped into my mind. I imagined myself hovering in the background, terrified she'd fall.

"How often should we use the callipers?" Rita asked.

"I'd recommend two or three times a day for around fifteen minutes, gradually increasing the time as she gets used to wearing them. After a couple of weeks of standing, we can move onto the next stage, which is getting her to take a few steps."

"How will we do that?" I asked.

"We'll teach her to lean to one side, and swing the opposite leg, using her arm and back muscles. Then she'll push the frame forward a little, lean towards the opposite side, and swing the other leg through. Progress will be slow, but she'll gradually improve."

I imagined Karen wending her way along the sidewalk to the local convenience store on the corner of our street. I returned her to the couch and, with Mr Strach's help, removed the callipers and boots.

"When she comes for her next appointment in three months, we'll try to get her to walk using the parallel bars in the physiotherapy department." Mr Strach waved us away from his office as he sat at his desk writing up Karen's notes with an old-fashioned fountain pen.

I pushed Karen back to the car park with Rita beside me carrying the callipers, the leather straps and metal buckles rustling as she walked. "How does he expect her to walk in this contraption?" Rita hefted the callipers and quickly let them drop as if they were too heavy to lift.

"We'll just have to see how she gets on, Rio. It won't be easy, but it's better than doing nothing at all."

Back at the car, I swept curling sycamore leaves from the windscreen while Rita strapped Karen into her seat. I opened the boot, folded the pushchair, and crammed it into the restricted space. Isolated raindrops began to fall, the prelude to a heavy shower. I started the car and quickly re-joined the Liverpool-bound traffic on the A57. The Morris Minor Series II had a two-piece windscreen with a chrome divider, and the wipers struggled against the sudden downpour.

Rita sat in the back and supervised Karen who was eating a jam butty. They chatted in baby-speak while I gave some serious thought as to how we were going to teach Karen to walk with Mr Strach's callipers. No magic solution sprang into my head. It would take time and lots of hard work.

We spent the following months getting Karen used to standing while holding the walking frame. At first, she was reluctant, but we persevered, offering soothing words and encouragement, and her confidence gradually increased. It wasn't long before she was able to stand against an armchair to play with her favourite toys, a rag doll named Sally and a one-eyed red-and-white teddy bear called Fluffy. She would forget she had the callipers on, and soon managed to stand unaided holding on to the walking frame.

This was achieved almost without Karen noticing. Holding on to her from the rear, I would stand her up to watch television. She particularly liked the Magic Roundabout, with Florence, Zebedee, and Dougal the dog. After a few minutes, Rita would move the Zimmer frame into position directly in front of Karen. I would then gently tip her forward, and she would instinctively reach for the frame for support. Little by little, I would release my grip on her until she was standing on her own.

We practiced this manoeuvre every day. Each time she stood unaided, I experienced a powerful emotion. It was more than pride. I was proud when I won the history prize at Quarry Bank High School. I was proud when I was presented with my school colours in football and cricket. This was different. The hair on my arms rippled as though charged with electricity. My heart rate increased. I felt energised with hope! Hope for a future where Karen would be able to join in children's games, go to school, go to work, become a woman, marry and have children.

My feelings ran deeper than normal parental love and pride. My daughter was a very special little girl, determined, brave, and irrepressible.

-0-0-0-0-0-

In December, we arrived back at Whiston Hospital for a scheduled session with a physiotherapist prior to Karen's next appointment with Mr Strach. We spent some quality time in a small gymnasium teaching Karen to walk in her callipers using height-adjustable parallel bars. With the help of the therapist, a young raven-haired woman named Rhonda, we helped Karen use the bars to take a few small steps. Rita and I knelt in front of her, just out of reach, and Rhonda hovered behind her. We urged Karen to lean to one side, and to swing her leg through a few precious inches by pulling on the bars.

"That's good, sweetheart. Good girl! Just a little bit more. Well done!" Cheering every tiny step, we encouraged Karen along from one end of the bars to the other. It took her fifteen minutes to walk ten feet, but she finally reached the end, and threw her arms out for me to catch her. I looked down at her. She was breathing hard after her exertions, and her plump cheeks glowed.

Rita ruffled Karen's hair. "Well done, Karen. You can walk! Isn't that great?"

We were shown into Mr Strach's office. He had followed Karen's progress during the last few minutes of her walk. I unlocked the hip and knee joints in her callipers and sat her on my knee.

"*Hurá*, Karen, well done!" Mr Strach squeezed her arm. Karen hid her face in her hands.

"Don't be shy, Karen. Say hello to Mr Strach," I said, pulling her hands from her face.

"Allo, Misstack," she ventured, attempting the difficult words.

Mr Strach knelt beside us, unlaced Karen's boots, and examined her feet. Karen reached down with a chubby finger and touched Mr Strach's bald spot. He looked up, smiled, and held on to her hand as he spoke to us.

"The tendons at the back of her lower legs are both a little tight, which is causing her feet to arch. She'll probably require an operation to correct this, but for the moment she is making good progress. I'll continue to see her every three months, and we will decide later if surgery is required. In the meantime, keep up the good work."

He leaned forward and kissed Karen on the cheek. "Goodbye, little One. See you soon. "Bye 'bye." He mimed an exaggerated wave.

We left in good spirits. It had been an uplifting experience to see Karen walking along the parallel bars, and we looked forward to her second Christmas, and beyond, with increased confidence. I felt she had made tremendous progress and deserved an extra-special present for her hard work. I had discovered an Edwardian doll's house in George Henry Lee's, which I was sure she would treasure. Somehow, I would find the money to buy it.

Karen continued to practice walking with her Zimmer, progressing with a slow, rolling gait. As I was working a three-shift system, I could spend time with her at different periods of the day, and Rita and I habitually fitted Karen's callipers for an hour each morning, afternoon, and evening, encouraging her to walk a little farther each time. The regime was tough on a two-year-old, and Karen didn't always want to practice, preferring to play with her toys, or wheel herself around in her trolley. In time, though, it became a part of her life, as commonplace as getting dressed in the morning.

-0-0-0-0-0-

At this time, I was working as a computer operator at English Electric on a rotating three shift basis. A few days before Christmas, after returning from the night shift and sleeping for several hours, I got up and pulled on my jeans, finding the house unusually quiet. I pushed open the lounge door and a scene of devastation confronted me. The budgie's cage was lying on its side, its door wide open, and the carpet was shrouded in blue and white feathers.

I called out to Snowy. "Here kitty, kitty…" Not a meow… not a purr.

I called out to Billy, recently deprived of his plumage. "Here Billy, Billy…" Not a whistle. Not even a tweet.

I looked in every nook and cranny, but there was no sign of either the victim or the culprit. Searching again, I moved the sofa from the wall and found a small round ball. I picked it up. It was soft and fluffy and, as I turned it over in my hand, I noticed a tiny yellow beak.

I knew the cold-hearted killer was somewhere in the room because the door had been shut when I first arrived on the scene. I searched again, standing on tip-toe to pull down an old shoebox from a high cabinet. Inside, sound asleep, was Snowy. He stirred as I lifted the box down, turning over on his back, inviting me to scratch his soft white belly.

My first instinct was to strangle him, but I soon realised that, in Snowy's eyes, Billy had been a juicy meal, not a pet budgie I had trained to say "Pretty Billy" and "Close that door". As I began to clear up the mess, Rita arrived home from shopping with Karen. She took in the scene with a horrified glance and made a beeline for Snowy—murder on her mind. "You little bastard, Snowy, I'll kill you!"

He was too quick, though, and, squirming through her legs, he was out of the door in a flash to the sanctuary of a thousand hiding places.

"Rio, take Karen outside while I clean up. Tell her Billy has flown away to heaven," I whispered. I would have to make up a new bedtime story featuring avian angels on fluffy white clouds.

The next day, asleep once more after a long night shift, I was awakened by a screech of brakes. Heart pumping, I jumped out of bed, pulled on my jeans and a knitted sweater, and flew down the stairs. I ran barefoot into the street, eyes squinting, toes curled against the cold pavement.

A lorry was stationery in the middle of the road. Behind the wagon, ground into the tarmac, was a red and white furry splotch. The lorry driver climbed down from his cab to inspect the damage. "I didn't see him, mate," he apologised.

"Don't worry about it," I replied, "He deserved it." *What goes around, comes around.*

The driver scratched his head and climbed back into his cab. I went back into the house, returned with a shovel and a cardboard box, and scraped Snowy's remains from the tarmac.

Tonight, Karen's bedtime story would have a different ending.

Five

Christmas has always been my favourite time of the year, even during the late 1940's, when the only gifts in my stocking would be a compendium of board games, a Beano annual, and a tangerine. Life in post-war Edge Hill was tough. We had lived in an area surrounding the Cameo picture-house often referred to in the *Liverpool Echo* as Murder Mile, but my memories of our little terraced house on Bective Street were of a childhood replete with fun and laughter, and a great camaraderie among our neighbours. The area abounded with colourful characters such as Mr Mac, the gas-lamp lighter, Polly Brown, the sweet shop owner, custodian of the neighbourhood's secrets, and Mr Peagram, the local chandler, known to everyone as Mr Pea.

In Hans Road, Walton, where we lived in December, 1967, we also had our share of eccentric characters, like our next-door neighbour, Mrs. Hughes. She appeared to be a perfectly normal old lady during the day, but as soon as darkness descended, she morphed into a ranting, cursing maniac. Night after night, the diatribe would go on:

Get off me, you f***in' demon, get off me. If my Albert were here you wouldn't talk to me like that. F*** off…

Every curse could be clearly heard through the thin walls. I decided to have a word with her, and on Christmas Eve, a little before dusk, I knocked on her door. I was carrying a bottle of Harvey's Bristol Cream wrapped in festive gift paper. She opened the door a crack, peeped out, then opened it wide. "Oh, Davie, it's you…"

"Merry Christmas, Mrs. Hughes." I thrust the gift into her hand.

"A present for me? Oh, Davie, thank you." She grinned and displayed toothless gums. She threw a scrawny arm around my neck and tried to snog me with slobbering lips. I turned my head and her kiss skidded off my cheek.

"Mrs. Hughes, will you do me a favour? Please don't swear so much. We can hear every word you say through the walls. I don't want Karen to hear these words."

"But, Davie, the devil visits me every night. He tries to do the most awful things to me."

"I'm sorry about that, Mrs. Hughes, but there's no need to use such foul language."

"He's in there now, Davie."

"Who?"

"The devil."

"Just ignore him and he'll go away. Have a glass of sherry and forget about him."

"I'll try, Davie."

I ushered her back inside the house and her vicious, evil-eyed cat, with its black matted fur, rubbed itself on her legs as she shuffled back indoors. I hadn't forgotten the claw marks on my back.

When I got back to my house, I found Karen standing in her callipers. She held onto her walking frame as she watched *Magic Roundabout* on television. I crept up behind her and kissed the top of her head. She looked up and her eyes gleamed with delight. "Zebee, Dad." She pointed to her favourite character on the screen, holding on to the Zimmer with the other hand. Her balance and confidence had improved to such an extent we could leave her alone for a few minutes without fear she would fall.

"What's Zebedee doing, sweetheart."

"Play Doogull."

"He's playing with Dougal, is he?"

"Doogull say woof, woof."

"Dougal says woof, woof? Isn't he a clever dog?"

In a corner of the lounge, a Norwegian spruce twinkled with fairy lights and silver tinsel; packages wrapped in Christmas paper were heaped around its base. The mouth-watering smell of freshly-baked mince pies wafted through the house.

"Dave," Rita shouted from the kitchen. "Take Karen's callipers off, will you, please? Her dinner's nearly ready."

"Jawohl, mein Führer!" I shouted back, goose-stepping towards Karen with a finger laid across my upper lip. Karen giggled, as I knelt on the floor beside her. "Let's take your callipers off, sweetheart. You've had them on a long time, today."

I held her around the waist, pushed the Zimmer out of the way, and laid her on her back. I quickly unbuckled the leather straps and removed the heavy harness. Angry red welts were imprinted on each thigh, and I massaged them with Johnson's baby oil until the marks had faded. I sat Karen in her highchair and clipped the plastic tray to the front. Rita came in from the kitchen with our daughter's dinner, a mash of potatoes, carrots, turnips, marrowfat peas, and Bisto gravy.

After Karen had eaten her dinner and drunk her milk from a plastic beaker with a toddler-friendly mouthpiece, I cleaned up the debris and wiped a mess of food from her face and hands. She had been spoon-feeding herself for a number of months now, an early sign of the independent spirit we were determined to instil and nurture.

Later, when Karen was sleeping soundly, I crept upstairs to the spare bedroom and returned with a large box containing a self-build kit for a one-twelfth-scale Edwardian doll's house, which I needed to put together from the plan and materials supplied. Rita spent the evening baking a traditional Christmas cake, with sultanas, currants, and glacé cherries, topped with marzipan and smothered in white icing.

As I assembled the doll's house, an authentic replica of an imposing early 1900's residence began to take shape. It was double-fronted, with twin gables, mock-Tudor wood panelling, and distinctive square bay windows. The roof hinged backwards to reveal four rooms adorned with period furniture. By the time the glue had set on the last panel, it was nearly midnight.

Rita had gone to bed a little earlier. She had been baking for most of the day, and plates of mince pies, dusted in icing sugar, were laid out on the dining table alongside a Christmas cake, adorned with a plastic snowman and a sprig of holly. I covered the doll's house in gift-wrap, placed it alongside the Christmas tree, and retired.

Mrs. Hughes had remained eerily silent throughout the evening. I guessed she'd drunk herself comatose on the bottle of sherry I'd given her.

-0-0-0-0-0-

Christmas Day, 1967, dawned cold and clear. Last Christmas, Karen had been just seven months old, and she hadn't understood the significance of Christmas. This year we had taken her to see Santa Claus at the grotto in Blacklers department store. Looking slightly bewildered, Karen had been photographed sitting on Santa's knee and had received a present, a box of Rowntree's *Jelly Tots*. She now associated Santa Claus with reindeer, sleighs, and sacks full of gifts. I had tried to teach her the names of Santa's reindeer but I could only remember Dasher, Donner and Blitzen, and, of course, Rudolph, with his nose so bright, Karen's favourite.

Karen was awake at seven, and I lifted her out of her cot and left her snuggled in Rita's arms in our bed while I ran downstairs to turn on the gas fire. I soon returned, shivering in my underwear. "Merry Christmas!" I managed through chattering teeth. "Shall we go downstairs and open our presents?"

Rita chorused, "Everybody say yeah!" and our baby daughter chirruped a reply.

Karen was wearing a fleecy bed coat which fastened at the bottom like a sleeping bag. I pulled on my jeans and crew-necked sweater, while Rita slipped on her dressing gown. I lifted Karen from the bed and carried her downstairs. The lounge had warmed a little, but it was still chilly. I sat Karen in her trolley and Rita joined us. "I wonder what's in that big parcel next to the tree?" I said to Karen. "Shall we go and see?"

She wheeled herself over, eyes wide with excitement. I helped her pull off the gift-wrap. She beamed as the doll's house was revealed.

"Santa's brought you a doll's house, Karen. Isn't it lovely?" Rita said.

"Sally's 'ouse," confirmed Karen. Her favourite rag doll had a home. I moved the model house toward the centre of the room where it was a little warmer. I placed it close to the fire and showed Karen how the roof hinged back to display the rooms beneath. She was fascinated with the model furniture. She picked up each miniature item in turn, inspected it carefully, and placed it back in position.

We spent the next half hour opening the remaining gifts from under the tree. Rita had bought me a bottle of Hai Karate after-shave and a hard-backed book, *The Naked Ape* by Desmond Morris, and I had given her the latest Kodak Instamatic camera. Karen received lots of presents from family and friends, including an Orphan Annie doll, educational games, picture books, including one of my favourites, *Rumpelstiltskin*, and a variety of clothes. She was spoiled, but she deserved it. She hardly ever complained about having to practice walking in her callipers.

The lounge was bedecked in festive paper chains and large decorative balls in warm shades of red, yellow, orange and green. A mass-produced print of a Vietnamese girl in traditional dress, which we had bought from Garston Market, hung over the fireplace, framed in gold and silver tinsel.

Rita draped Karen's Christmas clothes over the wire mesh fireguard to warm and, after a light breakfast of boiled eggs and toast, we bathed and dressed Karen in her new clothes. She looked as pretty as the Diego Velázquez painting of the Infanta Margarita in her pink satin dress and matching tights, an image only slightly tarnished by her plain brown walking boots. For today, like every other day, Karen would spend time standing and walking in her callipers.

I sometimes wondered if I was too strict on her when I forced her to walk for twenty minutes, three times each day, with heavy callipers. It broke my heart to see her struggle, and I constantly had to remind myself it was for her own good.

Rita and I took turns to strip-wash in the kitchen using water heated in the kettle. In the new year, I resolved to start the building project which would gain us a new ground-floor bathroom. I had spent the first seven years of my life bathing in a tin bath in front of the fire, so not having a bathroom was nothing new to me. However, I had become used to having a bathroom and indoor toilet during the interim years before I was married. Since buying our first house, it was back to basics, with no bathroom and an outside privee.

We spent the remainder of the festive period at my parents' house with Mum and Dad, my sisters Irene and Jean, and brothers Geoffrey and Barry. We exchanged gifts, enjoyed a sumptuous lunch of turkey, pork, and lamb, with all the trimmings, quaffed sparkling Italian wine, watched the Queen's speech on television, and dozed in front of the fire. What else did families do on Christmas Day?

-0-0-0-0-0-

In the New Year, I drew up my plans for a new bathroom on a ruled sheet of paper in a school exercise book, the kind that has metric conversion tables printed on the back. With only a plastic ruler and a rubber-tipped HB pencil I sketched my grand design. I intended to build the bathroom extension onto the existing kitchen, using the space in the back yard currently occupied by a wooden lean-to shed and the outside toilet.

I made a scale drawing of the quarry-tiled back yard, which was an inverted L-shape with high brick walls separating our property from the neighbours on each side. Another high wall at the rear contained a rickety wooden door, which led to a narrow, cobbled footpath, known colloquially as a "jigger."

My plan was to build a new wall stretching from the corner of the kitchen to the jigger wall, boxing in the part of the yard containing the shed and the toilet. I then planned to fit a wooden roof, demolish the shed and the toilet, and knock a hole in the adjacent kitchen wall to form an interior access door. Next, I would fashion a tongue-and-groove board floor on rough wooden joists, plaster the interior walls, install a new bathroom suite with a copper hot water cylinder, and the job would be complete.

My only qualification for undertaking this project was a GCE "O" level in Woodwork. Going strictly by the book, I should have submitted my plans to the City of Liverpool Surveyor for approval before commencing the work. However, this process could take up to six months, and I didn't want to wait.

Working almost entirely alone, I followed detailed instructions in a DIY manual and, using every moment of my spare time, two months later a new bathroom, with a gleaming white bath, toilet and wash basin, and piping hot water, testified to my hard labour. The most difficult, and dangerous, job had been knocking out a doorway from the kitchen through the exterior load-bearing wall, but, with the help of Rita's dad, Sylvester, and an old railway sleeper used as a lintel, even this tough job was completed without resorting to expensive tradesmen.

Karen's first bath in the new bathroom was a huge pleasure for her and for me. She sat surrounded by soapy bubbles and we had a pretend fight, covering each other's faces with foam in the process. Rita and I could now look forward to long soaks in our own bath, alleviating nightly strip-washing and twice weekly visits to the local public baths.

While building the bathroom, I had an opportunity to repay Mrs. Hughes" cat for the scratches on my back. I was sitting on an upturned breeze block drinking tea, when the flea-infested feline with the feral eyes came into view. He sat on my new roof, like a monarch surveying his kingdom. I placed my mug on the ground and, moving slowly, picked up a lump of mushy cement. As I stood, arm drawn back to launch the sloppy missile, the cat saw me, arched his spine, and hissed. I let fly and—*splat*—hit him full in the face. He squealed and ran around in circles, shaking his head from side to side. Flecks of cement flew in all directions before he disappeared into his own back yard, mewling and yawping like he'd been peppered with shot.

That night, the cat's eyes would be more red than yellow. I hoped he'd learned his lesson and would stay well clear of me in future, but more importantly, I wanted the cat to stay away from Karen when we sat her outside in her pram.

Once the bathroom was complete, I wrote to the City Surveyor's office to have it approved, and a few weeks later a surveyor from the Liverpool Corporation planning office arrived to inspect the building and plumbing. He was tall and thin and wore a beige Gannex raincoat. He carried a clipboard and made notes as he inspected the building. He was surprised I hadn't sought planning permission before the work had started. "Do you realise, Mr Verinder, I could order you to demolish this building?" he asked with the haughty bureaucratic air of a career civil servant.

I shook my head and looked suitably worried, holding my breath as he peered at his notes

"I'm going to approve the extension with one condition. You will have to build an interior airlock between the kitchen and bathroom. According to Council regulations, you have to have at least two doors between a kitchen and a toilet."

I let out my breath. "That's no problem. I'll get onto it right away."

-0-0-0-0-0-

Karen's second birthday coincided with the Beatles' *Hey Jude* reaching number one in the music charts and, like Liverpool's most famous sons, she had come a long way in a short time. Weather permitting, she was now allowed to play outdoors in her trolley. After a year of practice, she handled her trolley with considerable prowess, negotiating obstacles like an Olympic downhill slalom skier. To allow her to safely climb kerbstones, I modified the trolley by screwing a small castor to its base at the back to prevent it from tipping over. By leaning backwards, Karen could tip the trolley sufficiently for the front castor to clear the curb, then she would push hard on the wheels, forcing them up and over the edge of the pavement.

Rita and Karen established a routine. Each afternoon around four o'clock, they would go to the local convenience store to buy the *Liverpool Echo*. Karen would have to cross two roads in her trolley to reach the corner shop. On reaching the store, Karen reached up and knocked on the window with a coin. A shop assistant would bring out the *Echo* and a lollipop or penny chew for Karen. Within a year, understanding the need to follow the highway code, she would go to the corner shop on her own, with Rita watching from the doorstep.

In August of 1968, we enjoyed our first family holiday in Weston-Super-Mare, a seaside resort in the county of Somerset, an area famed for its apple orchards and Scrumpy cider. With my cousin Pat, her husband George, and daughter Yvonne, who was just a few months older than Karen, we crammed into my Morris Minor and set off for the West Country, luggage piled high on the roof-rack. After a tiring six-hour drive, we arrived at the family-run Bella Vista Hotel, situated less than a hundred yards from the seafront, harbour and marine lake.

We left Karen's callipers and trolley at home—for two weeks she would be allowed to enjoy her first holiday without having to endure her strenuous daily exercise. Weston-Super-Mare, with its imposing Grand Pier and Theatre, exquisite Floral Clock, thatched limestone cottages, and donkeys on the sands, was a typically British coastal resort. It was also an ideal location from which to explore the nearby city of Bath, with its Roman spa and temple, and the village of Cheddar, famous for its cheese, ravine, and caves.

When we visited Bath, we learned the Romans had developed *Aquae Sulis* around natural hot springs, providing a sophisticated series of baths and a temple dedicated to the goddess, Minerva. Rita, Pat and the children preferred to explore the Guildhall Market, while George and I toured the historic Roman site. The tour was short, as the lure of the Grand Pump Room bar and Sheppy's Scrumpy Cider, brewed with local Dabinett apples, proved too difficult to resist. With an alcohol content of 7.2%, two pints each of the cool, delicious brew promoted a mood of sparkling conviviality for the remainder of the day.

Our visit to Cheddar Gorge and Goughs Cave, with its cathedral of caverns formed by Ice Age melt waters, was particularly memorable. As we entered the vast Diamond Chamber, a uniformed female attendant approached me. "Excuse me, sir, would you mind taking your daughter out of the pushchair and letting her walk for a few minutes. The path ahead is too narrow for prams and pushchairs."

"Do you believe in miracles?" I asked with a smile.

"No, sir, why do you ask?" Her brow was furrowed.

"She can't walk. Her legs are paralysed." I lifted Karen out of her pushchair and handed her to Rita, while I folded it up.

She reddened. "Oh, sir, please forgive me. I didn't know. She looks just like any…"

"Please, don't worry. You couldn't possibly have known."

As George led Yvonne around by the hand, I carried Karen and allowed myself a short moment of reflective sadness. I hugged my daughter as she pointed to a group of spot-lit stalactites hanging from the roof of the cave.

"Look, Dad, teeth!"

"Yes, sweetheart, giant's teeth." I kissed her cheek. *How I loved this adorable little girl.*

-0-0-0-0-0-

On a cold December morning, four months after our holiday in Somerset, we set out once more to Whiston Hospital for our latest appointment with Mr Strach. After a short wait, Rhonda, the physiotherapist, beckoned us into the small gymnasium, where Mr Strach stood reading Karen's medical notes. I carried Karen and Rita carried Karen's walking frame.

"Hello, Karen," Mr Strach said, as he looked up. "You look very smart in your new pink coat." He took Karen's plump little hand and kissed it. "Okay, let's see how you can walk."

I removed Karen's quilted winter coat, which was oversized to allow for her callipers, and placed her on the parquet-tiled floor between the rubber handles of her Zimmer. "Show Mr Strach how you can walk, sweetheart."

Karen pushed the Zimmer forward a little, leaned to the left, and swung her right leg about ten inches ahead. Then, leaning to the right, she swung her left leg forward ten inches. She repeated this process and gained a steady momentum. Mr Strach walked at the same pace on Karen's left and Rhonda walked on her right. Karen walked the width of the gymnasium, a distance of approximately thirty feet. Then, inching the Zimmer through 360 degrees, she turned and walked back.

"*Dobře*, Karen, well done!" Mr Strach beamed.

"Let's go into my office." He led the way. I picked Karen up and Rita carried the Zimmer.

"See you soon, Karen, 'bye, darling," said Rhonda. Karen waved shyly.

Mr Strach asked me to lay Karen on a treatment couch and take off her callipers. He then examined each of Karen's feet in turn, massaging them and flexing her ankles. He shook his head and delivered the bad news. "I'm afraid Karen will need an operation to stretch the tendons at the back of her lower legs, otherwise the increased arching of her feet will make it difficult for her to continue to walk in her callipers."

Rita closed her eyes and pursed her lips. I squeezed her hand.

"Look here." He lifted Karen's right leg. "Her right foot has a tight Achilles tendon, which is causing her foot to point downwards. We will correct this by elongating the tendon to make it looser and provide a greater degree of flexibility in her foot." He drew an imaginary line down the back of Karen's lower leg with his index finger.

He lowered Karen's right leg and raised the other. "Her left foot is pointing outwards due to tightness in one of the peroneal tendons, which again we will correct by stretching and elongating the tendon." He illustrated again with his finger, before lowering her leg.

"How long will she be in hospital?" Rita asked.

"For seven to ten days. As soon as we remove the stitches we will discharge her."

"Will her legs be scarred?" I asked.

"She will have hairline scars from the base of each ankle at the back of her leg up towards the calf muscle. They should heal quickly and be hardly noticeable." Mr Strach moved around his desk and sat down to write up Karen's notes. Rita lifted Karen from the couch and sat opposite Mr Strach with Karen on her knee. I stood behind her, holding Karen's callipers. I stared at the anatomical poster on the wall behind Mr Strach's head and marvelled at the complexity of the human body.

Mr Strach consulted his diary and scribbled a note. "We will schedule the surgery for Friday, the fourteenth of March. My secretary will confirm this in a letter."

He looked at Rita's troubled face.

"Don't worry, Mum, Karen will be fine. The operation is routine."

Six

On Thursday, January 9, 1969, the city of Liverpool was brought to a virtual standstill by the worst freezing fog in living memory. My homeward journey from work, through the normally frenetic Queens Drive traffic, had taken more than an hour instead of the usual twenty minutes. Nevertheless, I had returned home safely, eaten dinner, and was watching television, with Karen sitting on my lap. She'd already had her bath and her skin shone with a healthy pink glow. Rita had left for an evening shift at the Sayers confectionary factory. The extra money she earned had helped to finance our new bathroom.

The opening bars of the *Top of the Pops* theme music blared from the television, and soon the flashing neon-sign logo gave way to a cheering crowd of young people gathered around a central stage. The camera zoomed up to a metal gantry and zeroed-in to a head-and-shoulders shot of Jimmy Saville, the zany, bleached-blonde presenter. "Ladies and gentleman, guys and gals, welcome to Top of the Pops!" He waggled his trademark Havana cigar next to his mouth. "Tonight, we have Fleetwood Mac, Marmalade, and Scaffold in the studio, but to open the show, please give a great Top of the Pops welcome to The Move and their new single, *Blackberry Way!*"

The young studio audience roared its appreciation. Roy Wood, the lead singer with the long wispy beard, stepped into the spotlight and mimed to the record. The crowd swayed and danced to the beat. I bounced Karen on my knee and we clapped along.

She pointed to the screen. "Santa, Dad."

I laughed. "No, not Santa, sweetheart. Santa's beard is white."

The Move finished their spot and the garrulous presenter ran through the Top Twenty in reverse order, introducing the featured artistes as he reached their appropriate position in the chart. Marmalade performed a cover version of the Beatles album track, *Ob-La-Di, Ob-La-Da*, and Fleetwood Mac, with Stevie Nicks on vocals, performed *Albatross*. They were joined by Amen Corner, Joe Cocker, and the Hugo Montenegro Orchestra.

Finally, Saville announced the number one record. "For the fourth week running, guys and gals, the number one best-selling record in the UK is... *Lily the Pink* by Scaffold!"

The Liverpool folk group—Roger McGough, poet, John Gorman, comedian, and Mike McCartney, brother of the Beatles' bass guitarist— stood shoulder-to-shoulder on the stage. Karen loved this song for its uncomplicated tune and lyrics. The simple opening guitar riff gave way to the chorus, to which Karen and I sang along:

We'll drink, a drink, a drink,

To Lily the Pink, the Pink, the Pink,

The saviour of the human race,

For she invented medicinal compound,

Most efficacious in every case.

The song was a parody of Lydia Pinkham, the famous American nineteenth century alchemist, whose vegetable compound, according to an advertisement in the *Salt Lake Weekly Herald* in December, 1881, was reputed to cure a range of feminine complaints "from ovarian tumours to fainting and flatulence." Not a lot of people know that, as Michael Caine might have said.

After Top of the Pops, it was almost Karen's bedtime, but there was just enough time for me to run through the home-made flash cards I had devised to help her learn to read. I held up the first card. On it was a crude drawing of a cat, closer to L. S. Lowry's matchstick style than a Diego Velázquez portrait. Alongside the caricature, the word "cat" was written in large lower-case letters. On the reverse side of the card was the word without the drawing.

"C... A... T... spells..." I prompted.

"Cat," she replied.

"Very good." I turned over the next card. "And D... O... G... spells..."

"Dog."

I ran through the complete batch. When I had finished, I shuffled the cards and turned them over so this time Karen would see them without the drawings. I went through them again and she scored a perfect ten.

-0-0-0-0-0-

As the date for Karen's surgery approached, I wondered how she would react to being in hospital, separated from Rita and me for the first time in her recollection. She was sure to be upset, but I also wondered how Rita and I would cope. There would be a huge void in our life without our baby daughter.

We arrived at the Whiston Hospital admissions unit on the afternoon of Thursday, March 13, 1969. Karen's operation was scheduled for the following morning. After a bored receptionist had completed the paperwork and I had signed a surgical consent form, a uniformed porter escorted us to the children's orthopaedic ward. Karen enjoyed her ride down the main hospital corridor in a grossly oversized wheelchair. She read her *Goldilocks* book as we ambled along. "Look, Dad… baby bear."

"Yes, love. He's blowing on his porridge." My stomach began to flutter. We hadn't told her she wouldn't be coming home with us.

The porter turned into the orthopaedic ward and stopped outside the ward sister's office. The sister came out to greet us, and the porter handed her a manilla folder with Karen's name printed on the front. "So, this is Karen," she said, ruffling Karen's soft golden hair. "I'm Sister Howarth. How are you, sweetheart?" Our little girl turned away, smiling, her shyness endearing. "We'll take you to your bed now, shall we?"

Rita and I, together with the porter and his precious cargo, followed Sister Howarth down the ward, passing children, large and small, in beds and cots, some sleeping, some reading, some playing with toys. None looked pleased to be in hospital. Clipboards, containing the patients' temperature and pulse charts, hung on the end of their beds.

"This is your bed, Karen," Sister Howarth said, indicating an empty bed. "Mum and Dad can stay with you for a while." The first sign of puzzlement creased Karen's brow. I sat her on the edge of the bed, and the porter pushed the empty wheelchair back down the ward. "Mrs. Verinder, will you please undress Karen now and put her pyjamas on. You can store her clothes in the locker next to the bed. I'll come back in a few minutes." The sister went back to her office.

"This is nice, Karen," Rita said. "Look at the lovely drawings and paintings on the wall. Maybe you can draw one and we'll hang it over your bed." Rita pulled a colouring book and crayons out of a W. H. Smith's carrier bag and laid them on the bed next to Karen.

"Want to go 'ome, Dad," Karen said. Her eyes roamed from bed to bed as she noted the children tucked up tight.

"We'll go home soon, sweetheart. First, we have to see Mr Strach. You remember Mr Strach, don't you?"

Rita began to unbutton Karen's dress. "Don't want jamas on, Mum."

Karen's eyes were becoming moist, her manner agitated.

"All the other children have their pyjamas on, Karen," I soothed.

"Don't want jamas on, Dad." Her bottom lip trembled and she began to cry.

"I know, sweetheart, but you have to. Hush now, sweetie." I kissed teardrops from her face.

"Don't... want... jamas... on," she sobbed. Rita pulled Karen's dress over her head and replaced it with a Rupert Bear pyjama top. I lifted our distressed daughter a few inches off the bed as Rita pulled the matching pants over Karen's pink polka-dot underwear. "Want to go "ome, Dad, want... to... go... "ome." Her body convulsed with each sob. I picked her up and propped her against the pillows.

"When Mr Strach has seen you, love. Let's do some colouring." I lowered the adjustable bed tray and pushed it up close to Karen's chest. I opened the colouring book and box of wax crayons and placed them on the tray. "Look, Karen, a farmyard! What colour shall we use for the farmer's hat?"

"B... b... blue." Her sobs subsided and I passed her the blue crayon. In my peripheral vision, the ward sister beckoned Rita to join her. They whispered for a few moments and Rita returned to the bed.

"Mummy's just going to the toilet, Karen," she said, kissing her cheek. Then she whispered in my ear, "Dave, we have to go now." Rita moved away from the bed.

The sister approached. "That's a lovely picture, Karen. Can I help you to finish it?" I took my cue to leave, as the sister's body shielded me from Karen's view. I was halfway to the door when her cries resumed with increased intensity.

-0-0-0-0-0-

The following morning, we returned to the hospital at nine o'clock, as arranged with Sister Howarth. As we walked down the centre of the ward, a nurse emerged from the screens surrounding Karen's bed. "You must be Karen's mum and dad," she said. "Karen's sleeping now, but you can sit with her. I gave her a mild sedative about half-an-hour ago. She will be going to theatre in about fifteen minutes."

I pushed open the drapes. Karen lay flat on her back snoring softly; her cheeks flushed a deep rosy pink. She now wore a green gown. Rita and I sat on grey plastic visitor's chairs on either side of the bed. We each held one of Karen's hands through the raised metal sides. A "Nil by Mouth" sign was tied to the head of the bed with thin red tape. "She looks too hot," Rita said, loosening the gown a little at Karen's neck.

I heard the sound of squeaking rubber wheels on the parquet-tiled floor and guessed it was time for Karen to go to the operating theatre. The drapes swished back and a theatre nurse, dressed from head to toe in surgical green, stood alongside a gurney.

Rita and I stood and moved out of the way. The nurse lowered one side of the bed, pulled the single white sheet back, and gently supported Karen at the back of her neck and under her knees before lifting her onto the gurney.

At this point, Karen opened her eyes and looked into my face. "Take me "ome now, Dad," she slurred.

"Yes, sweetheart, I'll take you home." Her eyes closed again.

I held Karen's hand as the nurse wheeled her down the ward. At the door, Rita and I each kissed Karen's cheek, and then she was gone.

We waited at Karen's bedside for her return, and two hours later she was wheeled back into the ward and lifted into her bed by the same nurse who had collected her earlier. Karen was unconscious; bandages swathed her lower legs and feet. An hour later, as she came around from the anaesthetic, she asked for a drink. Rita went to the nurses' station in the middle of the ward and returned with a plastic cup containing a few ice cubes. She picked up a large cube and rubbed it on Karen's parched lips.

"Feel sick, Mum," Karen whispered.

"Dave, ask the nurse for a bowl, please. Quickly!"

I ran to the nurses' station. As I approached, an overweight black nurse was locking a medicine cabinet with a key attached by a thin chain to her uniform. "Nurse, Karen feels sick... do you have a bowl, please?" I was a little breathless. The nurse picked up a stainless-steel kidney-shaped bowl, moved around the counter with a speed belying her size, and ran down the ward toward Karen's bed, her ample rear-end rolling and swinging like a ship in a storm.

She was just in time. Karen had started to baulk and, as the nurse lifted her head toward the bowl, a stream of clear phlegm gushed from Karen's mouth. "Don't yo worry." Her voice boomed like a Rastafarian momma. "It's normaaal for a chile to be sick after anaesthesia. She'll be orrrlright now." The nurse wiped Karen's lips with a tissue and took the bowl away. At walking pace, her backside reminded me of a sack of fighting ferrets. Karen went back to sleep.

In the afternoon, when she had recovered from the anaesthetic, Karen was able to sit against plumped-up pillows. I read from her favourite fairy tale book. "Once upon a time there lived a miller who had a beautiful daughter." Karen never tired of the story of *Rumpelstiltskin*. "The miller had to visit the king's castle, and, wishing the king to think he was very rich, he told him he had a daughter who could spin straw into gold. "Ah," said the king, "that is indeed a wonderful gift. Tomorrow you must bring your daughter to my castle, that she may spin some gold for me." Then the miller was afraid and wished he had not spoken..." I paused. Karen's brow was furrowed. "What's the matter, sweetheart?"

"My legs hurt, Dad."

I pondered on this for a second. Karen's tendons had been stretched, so she must be feeling muscle pain, transmitted along neural pathways that were supposedly gridlocked. Interesting. "I know, sweetheart, they'll be better soon." I continued with the fairy tale. "When the girl was brought before the king…"

Before I had reached the end of the story, Karen was snoring softly.

-0-0-0-0-0-

A little over a week later, Karen was discharged from hospital. The wounds at the back of her legs had healed and the stitches had been removed. As Mr Strach had promised, the hairline scars were barely visible. She returned for weekly visits to Rhonda, the physiotherapist, who massaged her feet and ankles to increase their flexibility, and soon Karen was walking in her callipers again.

To celebrate Karen's third birthday in May, we held a party for our family and friends. Karen had been quite taken by a toy washing machine and spin dryer in Rita's mail order catalogue. The Chad Valley Hoovermatic had a lever on the front to select "wash only" or "wash and spin," and a handle on the side to turn the drums. It looked exactly like the real thing, and we had bought it as a special birthday present.

The first visitor on the late afternoon of Karen's party was her close friend, Diane Hooper. Diane was an adorable little girl who lived just a few doors away from our house in Hans Road. Diane, a year younger than Karen, had Shirley Temple curls and an impish face. They would play together for hours with their dolls and toys. Diane toddled around in her mother, Alice's, high-heeled shoes, and Karen would follow behind in her trolley. Every time I saw them together, I had mixed emotions—happiness that Karen could take part in children's games, and sadness that she could not participate on equal terms. On balance, sadness always weighed more heavily.

As the other party guests arrived, Karen—standing in her callipers—greeted them at the door. "Nan, Granddad, it's my birthday! I'm three today."

"Happy birthday, Karen. What a beautiful party dress! You look gorgeous!" Mum's eyes sparkled.

Karen loved the companionship of being part of a large family, and I was prouder than a preening peacock as I watched her greet her guests.

Later I took her callipers off and transferred her to her trolley so she could play with her friend, Diane. They played with Karen's Hoovermatic, washing some old hankies and socks, spinning them dry, and washing them again. Pop records, from artistes such as Junior Walker & The All Stars, Johnny Nash, The Equals, and Sly & The Family Stone, blasted out from my Dansette record player. Rita had prepared a delicious finger buffet, with sandwiches and chicken drumsticks, and, of course, a birthday cake with three pink candles and *Happy Birthday Karen* scripted in fine pink icing.

I stood back from the crowd in the darkened lounge as the three candles were lit and everyone sang *Happy Birthday*. Rita held Karen in her arms and leaned close to the cake so Karen could blow out the candles.

Exactly three years earlier, I had been alone, wracked by an emotional pain so intense it had made me physically sick. Today, my heart was brimming with happiness.

-0-0-0-0-0-

Soon, spring gave way to the summer of '69, and a young Canadian by the name of Bryan Adams was contemplating buying his first real six string from a five-and-dime on Vancouver Island. On the other side of the world, in Liverpool, the sun was rising on a cloudless Friday morning in July. My last night shift of the week at United Biscuits was just an hour from completion. My thoughts wandered to the narrow country lanes, rolling hills, and cool blue waters of the Cumbrian Lake District, where Rita, Karen, and I were to spend the weekend in a cabin on the shores of Lake Windermere.

I pressed the release switch, and the rising sound-proof hood of the gargantuan IBM 1403 printer unleashed a chattering burst of sound. Whirling metal type-heads bombarded continuous green-lined computer stationery, drowning out my rendition of *Honky Tonk Woman*. The last page of stationery squirmed under the type-heads and the noise level dropped by a zillion decibels. I pressed the red button to turn off the powerful drive-chain motors and tore open a new box of paper.

"Shut up or take singin' lessons, you little prick," Alan Webster, my workmate and beer-drinking buddy, shouted from his position at the 360/40's flashing console. I gave him the finger and invited him to swivel on it.

I was inserting the leading sheet of a fresh box of stationery onto the guide sprockets of the printer when a hammering on the computer-room door demanded my attention. Through the glass, a uniformed policeman urgently mimed the motion of a turning key.

Oh, no! Something's happened to Karen! Images of flashing lights and speeding ambulances flooded through my mind.

I ran to the door and pressed the rocker switch. The magnetic lock released, emitting a sound like swarming bees. As the door swung open, my heart tried to beat its way out of my ribcage. "What's wrong?" My tongue felt too big for my mouth.

"Have you been here all night?" the policeman asked.

"Yes, since eleven o'clock."

"Did you see or hear anything unusual?"

"No, nothing special. What's the problem?"

"There's been a robbery."

My heart rate throttled back a few thousand revs. "What? Someone's pinched some Jaffa Cakes?" He gave me a look that said *smart-arse*.

"The safe's been robbed. Don't leave the room. The robbers are armed and may still be on the premises." He turned and ran back in the direction of the safe.

Alan hovered behind me. "What's goin' on?"

"There's been an armed robbery. Someone's broken into the safe!" I said.

"No shit!"

We had walked through the darkened general office several times during the night on the way to the toilet, each time passing the formidable walk-in safe. In addition to a sophisticated alarm system, immediately in front of the safe a weight-sensitive area of parquet-tiled flooring was marked with bold yellow lines, daring any would-be villain to invade its space.

The guys on the morning shift were due to arrive a little before seven o'clock, but I guessed they wouldn't be allowed into the building until the police had secured the crime scene. An hour later, a plain clothes detective knocked on the computer-room door. "Who are you?" he asked, as I let him in.

"Dave Verinder."

He looked more like a criminal than a cop—bullet head, eyes like flint, and a boxer's nose.

"I'm Detective Sergeant McAteer. I need a statement from you. Is there anywhere we can talk privately?"

"There's the tape library."

"That'll have to do." I led him behind a bank of tape drives, vacuum tubes swishing a catchy rhythm, into the glass-walled tape library. He told me to sit in the only chair, while he perched on the edge of the desk, large, looming.

My statement was brief; I had seen and heard nothing. He told me the weekly wages for the biscuit factory workers had been stolen. I thought of empty pay packets and disbelieving wives.

"You must have seen something. The safe is just around the corner."

"No."

"You expect me to believe that?"

"Yes."

"You're a fuckin' liar!"

I shook my head. He stared hard and long, but I didn't waver. I signed the statement containing the few words he had transcribed. "Can I go now?"

He leaned close, his breath smelling of cigarette smoke and last night's tandoori chicken. "You can go, but I'm not finished with you. Tell your mate to come in."

I strolled across the anti-static floor tiles to my co-worker, who was typing instructions into the computer's teleprinter. "Dog Breath wants to speak to you," I said.

He shrugged and got up. I replaced him at the teleprinter.

Ten minutes later, the morning shift crew came in. Everyone spoke at once, wanting to know what had happened. "I've already worked an hour's unpaid overtime," I said, handing over the job schedule to the shift leader, "and I'm going away for the weekend. *Adios amigos.*"

A uniformed policeman, stationed outside the computer-room, accompanied me to my car and searched it thoroughly, finding no cash, except a couple of green pennies which hadn't seen daylight in many a year. I told him to keep the change.

I drove home in my rusty Morris Minor, with its creaking semaphore direction indicators, ate a light breakfast of white toast and marmalade with Rita and Karen, and told them about the robbery. At ten o'clock I went to bed. I planned to sleep for a few hours before setting off for the Lake District. Rita woke me around two o'clock to tell me two detectives were downstairs. I pulled on my blue jeans and white tee, and trudged glue-eyed down the stairs. Karen was playing outside in her trolley; I asked Rita to take her to the corner shop for some sweets. "Don't worry. They probably just want to ask me a few more questions. Just give me ten minutes."

Dog Breath was sitting in my favourite armchair. He got right to the point. "I don't believe you didn't see anything in the vicinity of the safe. The gang was helped by someone on the inside, and we think you were involved."

"Don't be ridiculous. Do I look like a gangster?" I smiled sweetly.

"One of the security guards has confessed to turning off the alarms and leaving the safe unlocked. He's named you as an accomplice."

"What! I don't know any security guards."

"You're a liar! You play football with Jimmy Mercer. You're coming to the station with us." I had forgotten Jimmy worked for security. Shit!

"Are you arresting me?"

Dog Breath's colleague, sitting opposite on the settee, cut in, "No we're not arresting you, but we need you to cooperate with our enquiries. You said you didn't notice anything unusual during the night?"

I nodded.

"The gang must have been in the safe for quite some time because more than seventeen thousand pounds was stolen, much of it in silver and copper coins, yet you maintain you saw nothing. How many times did you pass the safe on the way to the toilet?"

"Three or four times, I suppose."

"Was it three, or was it four?" Dog Breath again.

"It was probably three."

"When did you go?"

"I don't know, but I remember going once during my break, which would have been around three-thirty in the morning. I probably went once before and once after, but I can't remember the exact times."

"And you didn't notice anything, or see anyone in the area of the safe?"

"No."

"Would you mind if we searched your house?"

"Be my guest."

The two policemen looked at each other. My answers were consistent, and they appeared to reach a decision. Maybe they had already recovered the stolen cash and the gang was in custody.

Dog Breath's sweeter-smelling partner said, "We're sorry to bother you, Mr Verinder. There's no need for you to come to the police station at this time, although we may want to interview you again."

"No problem, but there's nothing else I can tell you."

A few minutes after I'd shown them out, Rita returned with an early edition of the *Liverpool Echo*. The headline on the front page blared— Armed Robbery at City Factory!

I read the report by the *Echo* crime writer. A gang of six hooded men, with local accents and sawn-off shotguns, had broken into the security lodge at the factory gates, and tied up the three guards. They had opened the safe without triggering the alarm system and had stolen nearly eighteen thousand pounds in cash. A security guard was under arrest on suspicion of aiding and abetting the gang.

Seven

The voice of astronaut Neil Armstrong travelled more than 240,000 miles through space to the Apollo 11 mission control centre in Houston, Texas, where it was transmitted to a world audience transfixed by the first manned lunar landing. Armstrong's Wapokoneta farming roots were revealed in his accent.

"Houston, this is Tranquillity Base. The Eagle has landed."

It was Sunday, July 20, 1969, and television pictures, beamed from the dusty surface of the Moon's Sea of Tranquillity, confirmed NASA's amazing achievement—man had finally landed on Earth's closest cosmic neighbour.

American astronauts had been rocketed to the Moon, yet, here on Earth, when my three-year-old daughter went to bed, she pulled herself upstairs on her forearms, slithering upwards like a human snake, dragging her lifeless legs behind her. I wondered what her prognosis might have been if the billions of dollars invested in the lunar space programme had been invested in spinal trauma research. I was becoming more and more troubled by Karen's disability, and for many months I was plagued by a recurring dream, so vivid I can describe it in absolute detail more than thirty years later.

The scene is Garston Parish Church where Rita and I were married. A beautiful young woman, with long golden hair, wearing a flowing white gown, is walking down the aisle on the arm of a man dressed in an immaculate dove-grey morning suit. The man has greying curly hair and resembles my father, but it can't be Dad because I can see the back of his head in the front pew. I realise the man walking down the aisle is me! The rows of old oak bench seats are packed tight with friends and relatives craning their necks for a view of the bride. Auntie Lil waves and I smile. I turn my head and glimpse three-year-old Karen behind us, struggling to keep up in her callipers and Zimmer frame. She is holding the bride's train in her teeth. We reach the front and the priest turns to greet us. It's Mr Isaacs, the vicar who conducted my marriage. I turn to the bride, lift her veil, and recoil in horror—a hideous human skull grins at me! Then, with a puff of smoke, the skull dissolves into dust and the dress crumples into a pile of dirty rags at my feet...

At this point I would be jolted awake, as though prodded with a live wire by a supernatural hand. My heart would be hammering in my chest, heavy beads of sweat on my brow. Then, the realisation it was only a nightmare would drift into my consciousness, and relief would flow through my body like floodwater into a storm drain.

Here's the reason I was so preoccupied: in two years, Karen would be five years old and ready to start school. The local primary school was located in Gwladys Street in the shadow of Goodison Park, home of Everton Football Club. As a lifelong Liverpool fan, I was more depressed than Grumpy at Snow White's funeral at the thought of Karen being educated in a school overlooked by the arch enemy. But, of course, there were more pressing reasons.

Whenever I contemplated Karen's schooling I would reflect on my own primary school days at Springwood County Primary…

I'm sitting at the front of the class alongside my mate, Charlie Hodgson, on a shiny wooden chair at a twin-pedestal desk covered in scrawled graffiti. Miss Naylor is explaining how tiny wriggling tadpoles emerge from a mass of frog's eggs called frogspawn to develop into slimy green baby frogs. As the tadpoles start to grow legs and lose their tails, she calls them froglets because they're no longer tadpoles and they're not yet whole frogs. It's so interesting, I don't realise my hand is in the pocket of my short grey trousers fiddling with my tiger's-eye marbles.

"Stop fidgeting and pay attention, David," Miss Naylor says. I feel my face flush with colour. She doesn't seem to know I'm listening to her every word, and she certainly doesn't know I love her. I haven't told anyone, not even Charlie. I think she knows I'm fond of her, but she doesn't know I love her almost as much as I love Mum and my sister. When I grow up I'm going to marry her as sure as tadpoles become frogs.

The lunch bell rings and chairs scrape against the waxed wooden floor tiles. "Children, put your books in your desks and walk quietly to the door. Don't run!" Miss Naylor shouts the last instruction. The classroom is filled with the noise of scuffling feet and banging desktops. As I jump to my feet and move away from my desk, I brush against Elspeth Peglar. She's nice to me when she's on her own, but when she's with her friend, Olive Hitchin, she pretends she doesn't like me.

Charlie and I are first out of the door, joining the kids from other classes as they pour into the corridor. We push and jostle our way through the crowd and skip down the three concrete steps into the playground. Charlie pulls a bare tennis ball from his blazer pocket and we begin our ritual fifteen-minute football game before lunch. We take turns to be goalkeeper in a goal formed by the gap between the boys' and girls' toilets at the bottom of the schoolyard. Soon we are joined by Brian Morgan, Tony Frith, and a group of other seven-year-old boys from our class. As I take my turn in goal, I notice a couple of younger kids rolling marbles, creeping behind the small coloured glass balls, shooing them towards their target marked in chalk on a paving stone. A gaggle of girls is skipping rope and chanting rhymes; others are playing hopscotch, and I can see Olive and Elspeth playing two-balls against the schoolhouse wall.

It's Miss Culshaw's turn for playground duty, and she wanders around, occasionally stopping to chat, on the lookout for what she calls "boisterous behaviour," which I think means fighting or arguing. Soon, she blows a whistle and all the kids scamper into lunch lines organised by class.

Charlie and I scramble into position near the front of our line. Miss Culshaw waits for the stragglers to take their places and then calls each class into the canteen starting with the youngest…

Then I imagine Karen in a similar classroom when the bell sounds. By the time she has pushed her chair back, locked the hip and knee joints of her callipers, and struggled to a standing position behind her Zimmer, the only other person in the room is the teacher. After three hours sitting in class she will no doubt need to visit the loo. I know Karen can't negotiate steps or stairs without help, but she might be lucky—there might be a toilet inside the school building at ground level within twenty yards of the classroom.

So, I imagine she's lucky and I go with her on a mental journey to the toilet. After shuffling and rolling her way down the corridor for five minutes, she reaches the door. The door opens inward, and she has no problem pushing it open and jamming it with her Zimmer while she drags herself through. She wends her way to a vacant cubicle, pushing the door open and manoeuvring the Zimmer inside. Now, she has to hustle the Zimmer through 360 degrees so she can sit on the toilet. If there's sufficient space for her and the Zimmer, she can close and lock the door, otherwise it stays open. Then she has to remove her underwear with one hand while standing upright and, after pulling herself onto the toilet, unlocking her hip and knee joints, and taking care of business, she has to reverse the procedure. By this time, the other kids have almost finished their lunch.

Despite my loathing of Everton Football Club, I went to Gwladys Street Primary School to check it out. What I found was depressing—no ramps, no wide doors, no inside toilets, no facilities whatsoever for a child with Karen's disability. On further investigation, it turned out there were no facilities in any regular Liverpool primary school that were entirely suitable for Karen.

There *was* a school in Sandfield Park, in the West Derby area of Liverpool, that catered exclusively for physically disabled children, but I wanted Karen to get the best education possible, and I didn't think she'd get it at a special-needs school.

"There's only one thing for it, Rio," I said. We were having breakfast on a late-summer Saturday morning. "We'll have to move."

"Move where?"

"I don't know. Somewhere near a suitable school." Karen was sitting in her high-chair eating a boiled egg with toasted bread soldiers. I leant over the table and wiped yolk from her face with a Kleenex.

"But, we're happy here," Rita protested.

"I know, love, but we have to find a school for Karen. I heard they are building a brand-new primary school on that new estate in Woolston where Irene and Chris live. We could take a look this afternoon."

My younger sister, Irene, had married Chris Hammond six months earlier, and they had bought a new house in Berkshire Drive, Woolston, a village on the outskirts of Warrington in Cheshire on the middle reaches of the River Mersey. Chris and I were great friends, more like brothers than brothers-in-law, having fought side-by-side in many teenage wars disguised as football games.

"I suppose there's no harm in looking," Rita said. "What do you think, Karen? Shall we go for a ride in the country? We might see some cows."

"And sheep… and lambs… and 'orses!" Karen pushed down with her strong arms, determination on her pretty scrunched-up face, and raised herself almost out of her seat. "Want to get down, Dad," she said.

"After you've finished your breakfast."

"But, Dad…"

"Finish you breakfast, young lady, or I'll tickle you until you beg for mercy."

I advanced menacingly with wiggling fingers, and she lowered herself back into her seat, flashing a dimpled grin to die for.

"Okay, Dad, okay! Please, don't tickle!" She raised her hands to ward me off, which I knew was an invitation to grab her ribs and tickle her until she squirmed and convulsed with laughter.

-0-0-0-0-0-

Under a clear powder-blue sky, we set off for Woolston in our beaten-up Morris Minor along the A57, which would take us from urban housing estates, through industrial areas of factories, breweries, and disused collieries, to the green serenity of rural Cheshire. Karen was strapped into her *Baby Care* seat in the rear, reading her nursery rhyme book, while Rita browsed through her *Woman's Own* magazine. Our route took us past Rainhill Lunatic Asylum, an austere nineteenth-century sandstone building with a square tower, set in immaculate landscaped grounds.

"Hey, Rio, have you heard the one about the Irishman walking past the lunatic asylum?" I asked.

"Not another one of your old jokes." She winced as if I'd let go a particularly nasty fart.

"Paddy is walking past a big wooden fence surrounding a lunatic asylum and, as he goes past, he hears the loonies chanting, 'Thirteen… Thirteen… Thirteen…' Paddy wonders what's going on, so he finds a small hole in the fence and looks in. As he bends toward the hole, one of the loonies pokes him in the eye with a stick and they change their chant to, 'Fourteen… Fourteen… Fourteen…'"

Despite her best efforts, Rita's face contorted into a grin, then into a spluttering laugh.

"What's a loonie, Dad?" Karen asked.

"It's a person who acts daft, sweetheart."

"Are you a loonie, Dad?" Out of the mouths of babes…

"Here's one for you, Karen. What wobbles, sits in a pram, and you can eat it?"

"Don't know, Dad."

"A Jelly Baby!"

Karen giggled and I had a captive audience for the next fifteen minutes, as I dredged up all the old jokes my Dad used to tell me when I was a kid. We made good progress past Bold Heath Colliery, through Warrington town centre, past a whiffy glue factory, and out into the countryside alongside Woolston New Cut Canal.

Eventually, I turned the old Morris off the A57 Manchester Road at Dam Lane, with the Rope & Anchor pub on the corner, and drove a final winding half-mile into Woolston. A road sign asked me to "Please Drive Carefully Through the Village", and I pulled into a vacant parking lot outside the post office. "Anyone fancy an ice cream?" I asked.

-0-0-0-0-0-

With Karen strapped into her push-chair, Rita and I sat on a wooden bench next to Ye Olde Village Cross and ate our ice cream cornets. Karen had more ice cream on her face than in the cornet, but we let her enjoy it in peace. The cross was hewed from a solid block of local sandstone and was mounted on a tapered circular pedestal. A burnished brass plaque declared the cross to mark the site of a Viking Round Tower Church, which was destroyed during the Norman Conquest.

We finished our ice creams and Karen's face was restored to its former impish beauty courtesy of Kleenex and her mother's spit. Leaving the car, we walked through the village and followed a sign down Warren Lane to a new John Maunders housing development. The building site was a mud-spattered scar on the otherwise pristine countryside. A large sign advertised "A development of sixty-four New English Rural Style houses, set in the heart of Cheshire in a place of great historical interest."

"What do you think, Rio? Shall we take a look?"

"We won't be able to afford one of these."

"How will we know if we don't go in and find out?" She shrugged. She was settled in our little terraced house in Hans Road and was wary of exchanging urban clutter for rural peace.

The route to the site manager's portacabin was a sea of mud with scattered islands of rain puddles. A meandering snake of wooden planks provided the only means of access through the mire. I unstrapped Karen from her push-chair, and hefted her into my arms, before venturing gingerly onto the first plank. I wobbled my way along the narrow makeshift path, with Rita following close behind, and reached the raised step outside the site office without mishap. I tried the door handle but it was locked.

We were just about to retrace our steps when I heard a scuffle inside the portacabin. I knocked on the door and, after a while, a key turned and the door opened. A huge man with the florid complexion of a country squire, tweed waistcoat straining against his prodigious belly, stood on the threshold. He had more chins than the Shanghai telephone directory and more spare tyres than the Michelin man!

"Sorry," he said, "we were closed for… er… lunch." I hoisted Karen high onto my right arm and glanced at the Timex strapped to my left wrist. It was almost 4 o'clock. He moved aside to let us in. A young girl pecked at a typewriter, head bowed, her face partially obscured by dark tumbling curls. The little I could see of her face was flushed a bright crimson.

"Sorry to disturb your… lunch," I said. "Is it okay if we look at the plans?"

"Yes, yes, sir, yes, of course," he stammered. "The site plan is on the wall and the brochures for the various house styles are on a shelf below the plan. If you need anything else, please just ask."

He retreated behind a grey metal desk covered with architectural plans and lowered his bulk into a dusty captain's chair. The telephone on his desk rang and he answered, "Maunders Woolston, can I help you?" Rita and I looked at each other. I arched my eyebrows and she stifled a grin. We wandered over to inspect the plans.

According to the site plan, the development would incorporate a primary school, which was scheduled for completion in the summer of 1971 when Karen would be five-years-old. As I transferred Karen to my left arm, she leaned down and picked up a brochure. The wall plan displayed a series of four T-shaped cul-de-sacs, each containing a range of semi-detached houses. The houses had fenced back gardens, but the front gardens were open-plan in the vogue of the late 1960's.

"Look, Dad, a dog." I glanced at the brochure Karen was holding. A model family—mother, father, girl, boy, and Old English Sheepdog—posed for the camera. The father was a rugged Rock Hudson type, his wife a wholesome Doris Day, and the children could have been plucked straight out of *The Sound of Music*. Rock was spraying his gleaming Ford Consul with a cascade of water from a hose, Doris was pruning roses, and the von Trapp children were romping on the lawn with the dog. In the background stood a Regency-style house, bay windows holding a lattice of small glass panes, some containing bubbles. It looked expensive.

"It's a sheepdog, Karen." The dog's long shaggy hair covered its eyes, a distinct disadvantage if it ever had to round up a flock of sheep.

I picked up a crudely stencilled pamphlet headed *Woolston Church of England Aided Primary School*. The single sheet of paper carried a dim photograph of a grimy Victorian building, the old school, and an artist's impression of the new school, a modern single storey building. A statement from the headmistress declared, "Our pupils are encouraged to develop an awareness of self and sensitivity to others, acquire a set of moral values, and develop habits of self-discipline and moral behaviour." It sounded more like a convent than a school.

We browsed for a while, collected a stack of brochures describing the various house models available and a price list, and left the site manager to finish his lunch.

-0-0-0-0-0-

The brochures were spread out on a coffee table. We were sitting in the lounge of my sister, Irene's, house in Berkshire Drive, a few hundred yards from the post office where we'd left our Morris Minor. Chris was working an overtime shift, and they could certainly use the money because Irene was five months pregnant with their first child. Karen was sitting on the floor playing a game with her favourite toys, Sally and Fluffy. Rita and I reclined on a settee and Irene perched on the edge of a matching chair.

"Irene, how much did your house cost?" I asked, dipping a ginger nut into my tea.

"It was three thousand three hundred and twenty-five pounds."

"How much deposit did you have to pay?"

"Let me think… It was ten percent, so that would have been erm… three hundred and twenty-five pounds."

"So, you got a mortgage for the rest?"

"Yeh, we got a mortgage from the Leeds Permanent Building Society." She sipped her coffee. "They'll advance up to three times your annual salary."

I did some quick sums in my head. "The cheapest of the houses we've been looking at is five thousand pounds. The new Church of England School is gonna be part of the estate, so it's perfect for us."

"If we can afford it," Rita chimed in.

"I'm due a raise soon, so maybe we can. There's no rush because they are still clearing the site. And it says here," — I waved the price list — "The houses will be released in four phases starting from the summer of 1970." I finished my tea and browsed through the glossies. Irene and Rita had moved onto babies' names and paid me no attention.

"I need a wee, Dad," Karen said, holding her arms out.

"Okay, sweetheart." I picked her up and carried her upstairs to the toilet. Obviously, she needed help with her underwear, and I realised it wouldn't be long before she would be too old for Dad to help her with such personal tasks.

Eight

In the autumn of 1969, Karen was fitted with bigger callipers. She was walking with much more confidence now, dragging herself around the house quicker and with more rhythm and continuity. However, some of the everyday things that the majority of people take for granted were a real effort for her. Opening a door towards her whilst in her callipers and using the walking frame was a long-winded and almost impossible task. The easiest course of action would be to open it for her but that would not help Karen in the long-term. She would have to find a way to do it herself. We would show her how it might be done but not do it for her.

It was heart-breaking to see our little girl struggling to do some of these everyday things but it was for her benefit that we let her struggle. We were determined she would become as independent as her condition would allow and if that meant watching her struggle to open doors then so be it. We had to become hard-hearted, which is not easy when your heart is full of love.

When she was not walking in her callipers, Karen was zipping around in her trolley or reading her story books. Every evening, except when I was working on the late shift, I would read the *Liverpool Echo* in my favourite armchair with Karen sitting on my knee. I encouraged her to read some of the headlines out loud.

Rita and I were delighted that Karen's mental capacity had not been impaired by her *hydrocephalus* condition. She was as bright as a full moon in a cloudless winter sky, with a sparkling personality that endeared her to everyone she met. Karen enjoyed an excellent quality of life despite her disability. She could walk... slowly, painfully, but she could walk. She could dash around the house and roam around the streets in her soap-box trolley which, ironically, was the subject of infantile green-eyed envy by the other neighbourhood children of her age.

A few years before Karen was born, Dad's sister-in-law, Joan, wife of his eldest surviving brother, Harold, had given birth to a Downs Syndrome child. Carl was a treasure, a remarkable boy as many children with his condition are, but he was very hard to handle and demanded constant attention. Uncle Harold, a top union official on Merseyside, was a very shrewd operator, a little eccentric, although some people might think him more pragmatic than unorthodox. For example, if Carl were to open a china cabinet and smash a few plates, Uncle Harold's solution would be to turn the heavy cabinet towards the wall, making it impossible for Carl to get at the crockery but... let's just say they used a lot of paper plates at mealtimes. Uncle Harold was a working-class hero, well known and respected throughout the City of Liverpool, but particularly among the thousands of militant dock workers. Unfortunately, his son, my cousin,

Carl, was to die before reaching his teens. I don't think I would have had the resolve to raise a child with a mental handicap.

-0-0-0-0-0-

The stepladder creaked alarmingly. Perched on top like a Golden Eagle in its eyrie, I stretched out towards the high ceiling with a lambskin paint roller dripping white emulsion onto the newspaper covered carpet below. Contorted, I reached for a tantalisingly out-of-reach corner. The ladder tottered but I regained my balance. I smiled as I realised the roller had reached into the tight angle, covering the last inch of dimpled plaster with hi-white Dulux. With the paint roller in one hand and the tray of paint in the other, I stepped down the ladder. Unfortunately, I had stepped off the side with no steps and crashed to the floor with hands flailing and a long "Oooooh, shiiiiit" escaping from my mouth. I landed on my back. The paint-tray hit the wall. The roller spun through the air and, in slow-motion, I watched it tumble towards Karen as she sat in her trolley. She had been reading a book when my shout and crash-landing grabbed her attention. Her mouth formed a perfect circle as the lambskin roller painted a white line down her nose before landing in her lap. She screamed and pushed frantically on the rear wheels, lifting the front castor into the air. She reached my side. "Dad! Dad!" she shouted. Winded, I couldn't respond. "Dad! Dad!" She shook my arm.

I turned my head towards her and winked. I regained my breath and started to laugh. I picked up the roller and painted a matching white line on my nose. Giggling, Karen swiped her finger over the roller and dabbed two white spots on my cheeks. I managed to get to my knees as Rita came into the lounge, arms loaded with shopping. "What the hell have you done?" she asked, surveying the damage.

"Oh, it's nothing," I spluttered. "We just decided to have a little fun."

"I can't leave you alone for a minute," she said, wiping Karen's face with a cloth.

I explained about my fall from grace and Rita checked out my back, which hurt like hell. "It's only bruised but it could have been worse—it could have been me!"

"Cheeky git! I could have broken my neck!"

After cleaning up the mess, I dressed Karen in her winter coat, gloves and hat and, with her snuggled up in her pushchair, we set off for County Road to buy some wallpaper while Rita prepared dinner. Everton were playing at Goodison Park on this Saturday afternoon and the surrounding streets were packed with cars. The glow from the floodlights lit up the early evening sky and the roar of the crowd sliced through the cold, damp air.

"Liverpool, Liverpool, Liverpool!" we sang in defiance to no-one in particular. "Hey Karen, did you hear about the Everton supporter who lost some books in a robbery? He was very upset because he hadn't finished colouring the pictures in!" I'm not sure if she understood but she laughed anyway. She was already well down the road to indoctrination as a Liverpool fan.

On the way home, rolls of wallpaper stacked up on the hood of the pushchair, we chatted. "What would you like Santa to bring you for Christmas?" I asked.

"Don't know, Dad."

"Well, I think you're getting a bit too big for your trolley. How about we ask him to bring you a bigger one?"

"Yes, please, Dad!" She spoke well for her age.

"We'll ask him next week, sweetheart, when we go to Blacklers' grotto."

The new trolley arrived just in time for Christmas. Her other presents were quickly forgotten as she scurried around the house singing along with Rolf Harris as he performed his Christmas number one record, *Two Little Boys*, on television.

-0-0-0-0-0-

The car stereo blasted out the latest Status Quo release... *rolling down the dust pipe now, got a ten-dollar bill in my jeans... because there ain't no room for a kosher cowboy in a town like New Orleans...* I imagined Francis Rossi and Rick Parfitt facing each other, only a few feet apart, guitars swinging in synchronised rhythm. Four-year-old Karen, strapped into her child seat, bobbed her head to the beat. Rita, elbows out, hands on hip, aped the famous Quo head-banging stomp, no mean feat when sitting in the front passenger seat of a clapped-out Morris Minor. We were en-route to Alder Hey Children's Hospital where Karen was to have a special x-ray of her waterworks.

The final strident chords of *Down the Dust Pipe* echoed from the speaker and were followed by the distinctive pips of the BBC time signal. "Good afternoon. It's two o'clock and this is BBC Radio News… Sectarian violence flared in Belfast today when soldiers shot dead a petrol bomber named as Danny O'Hagan. Troops were deployed in large-scale house-to-house searches in Catholic areas in a government crackdown on known activists. Newly installed Conservative Prime Minister, Edward Heath reiterated his determination to stamp out indiscriminate acts of violence in Northern Ireland…" Ted Heath, I mused. No doubt the latest in a long line of British Prime Ministers to break his election promises within a month of accepting office. The newscaster continued "… United States President, Richard Nixon, has authorised the blanket bombing of the Ho Chi Minh trail in Vietnam…" The world was a violent place in the summer of 1970.

Reporting to the Out-Patients Department at Alder Hey, we were sent to the Radiology Department, where we were met by a receptionist who took us into a green-walled ante-room, austerely furnished with a standard-issue National Health Service iron-grey metal desk, springy grey plastic chairs, and a grey leatherette examination couch. Shades of green and grey. That's how I remember the hospitals of the time. Directed by the receptionist, Rita took off Karen's clothes, dressed her in the inevitable green hospital gown, and we waited... and waited.

The door opened and a blonde woman doctor entered in a whirl of white coat, stethoscope, and steel kidney bowl containing a syringe and a phial of silver liquid. "Hello folks," she breezed in a soft North American accent. "My name is Patricia Donahoe. I'm a paediatric surgeon and urologist, and I will be examining Karen today using a procedure known as an IVP, which is a medical abbreviation for *intravenous pyelogram*."

"Sounds nasty," I said. "What is it?"

"It's essentially an x-ray examination of the urinary tract, including the kidneys and bladder, and involves the injection into the bloodstream of an organic dye, or *contrast medium*, to give it its correct term." Karen eyed the syringe and, sitting on my knee, gripped my hand with chubby but deceptively strong fingers. The doctor continued, "The dye passes through the kidneys where it is concentrated in the urine, casting a shadow which enables a specialist like me to view the urinary organs in absolute detail, identifying any abnormalities."

"How do you inject the dye?" I asked, holding my breath.

"It's just a standard intravenous injection into a suitable vein, usually in the arm."

I breathed out in relief. I had imagined it would be as painful as the *myelogram* procedure, where a dye is injected directly into the cerebro-spinal fluid through the spine. This was a simple intravenous injection. No problem.

Ms. Donahoe prepared the syringe, spiking through the seal of the phial and drawing the silver fluid into the calibrated plastic reservoir. I sensed Rita twitching in her seat. Karen's fingers tightened their grip. I hugged her. "Don't worry, sweetheart, this won't hurt. Just a little scratch and it will be over." Karen didn't seem convinced.

Taking Karen's hand and checking the veins in her wrist, the urologist tapped hopefully with the tip of a finger trying to identify a suitable vein. The only one I could see was a tiny blue tributary, more like a blood vessel than a vein. "Hold still, sweetheart," the doctor soothed as Karen squirmed in my lap. She attempted to break into the tiny vein and Karen cried out, almost launching herself out of my arms. No luck with that one. Doctor Donahoe tried another vein and I was forced to hold on tighter to my screaming daughter. *Prick.* No luck with this one either. She tried the other wrist, probing a little deeper, to increased howls of pain from the patient, and signs of extreme distress from the parents. Rita was so upset I asked her to wait outside. Karen was still crying hard when a vein suddenly popped out on her forehead, just above one of her eyebrows. Doctor Donahoe seized her chance and plunged the needle swiftly into the fat vein, injecting the dye with smooth dexterity

"There now, Karen. All done, sweetheart," she said as she extracted the syringe and dropped it into the kidney bowl. She placed Karen's tear-stained face in her hands and kissed her forehead. "I'm so sorry Mr

Verinder," she said, squeezing my arm. "It's usually such a simple matter, but Karen's veins sure are hard to find." She smiled and I forgave her. "Okay, let's get the x-ray done."

Carrying Karen in my arms, Doctor Donahoe led me to the x-ray room and I lay Karen face-down on the table. Her little body shook with tiny sobs. A young lady radiologist passed me a lead-lined apron so that I could comfort Karen during the remainder of the procedure. I held her hand and squeezed her sobs dry. The x-ray machine clicked and whirled, and I carried Karen back to the examination room, where Rita waited wringing her hands in torment. She jumped from her seat and grabbed Karen from my arms, hugging her fiercely and almost kissing her to death. Within a few minutes Karen was dressed in her street clothes and, except for heavy red-rimmed eyes, there was no evidence whatsoever of any kind of trauma.

Ten minutes later, Doctor Donahoe re-appeared with typical North American exuberance. "I'm pleased to say everything is just fine. No abnormalities." She joined her forefinger and thumb to create a circle of universal fineness, and we left.

The IVP experience led to Karen being pathologically terrified of needles and syringes for many years to come. The very mention of IVP would be enough to set off a panic attack.

-0-0-0-0-0-

We were soon approaching the Christmas holidays and, much to our delight, Karen was making excellent progress with her walking. Of course, she still struggled relative to other children of her age and it was distressing to see other youngsters running around effortlessly while she toiled so hard to take a few steps, but, nevertheless, there was discernible progress. Quite naturally, Karen preferred to be in her trolley, whether it be out in the street or indoors, because she could get around so much quicker.

Our daughter, miraculously, was now almost of primary school age and already she could read books aimed at seven-year-olds. Around this time, we started to notice that Karen's hearing was particularly acute. The slightest unexpected noise would startle her. Whereas most children loved to play with balloons, Karen hated them. She was terrified that they would explode and this phobia was never to leave her.

A few days before Christmas, we found ourselves back at Whiston Hospital to keep yet another appointment with Eric Strach, the charming Czechoslovakian surgeon who had become both a friend and talisman. Mr Strach and I watched from the side-lines as Karen displayed her walking prowess with callipers and elbow crutches while flanked by physiotherapist, Rhonda, and Rita. "She is walking with a good hinged gait," he observed. "She has good strength in her arms and upper back, and her progress is good."

"Yes, I'm really proud of her." Karen hauled herself around the gymnasium with slow, steady strides. "How did you end up in Liverpool, Mr Strach?" I asked him when the conversation flagged.

"I was born and raised in Prague and studied medicine at university. When the Second World War broke out and Germany invaded my country, I made my way to Paris and joined the Czechoslovakian Army in Exile. Then France fell to the Germans, and I was shipped to England with the Czech Army, landing in Liverpool." He winced at the painful memory. "After a year or so, I was released from the Army to work in local hospitals, including Alder Hey Children's Hospital."

"So, you stayed in Liverpool after the war?"

"Yes. I met my wife, Margaret, in Liverpool. At the end of the war, I volunteered to join a group of health workers in a German concentration camp where a typhus epidemic was raging. The Terezin Ghetto was situated just north of Prague and was populated by 140,000 Jews during the course of the war, many of them destined for Auschwitz and other extermination camps."

"It must have been horrific," I said.

He nodded. "Terezin was touted by Hitler as a paradise Jewish City, where prisoners led a full life and enjoyed many luxuries including classical music concerts. The reality was quite different. Conditions were hideous, with overcrowding and poor food, sanitation and medical care. Of the 140,000 people interned in Terezin during the war, 33,000 died and 87,000 were transported to Nazi death camps."

"How awful!" I winced.

His face was grim. "Only one in ten of the children interned at Terezin survived the ordeal." He looked whimsically in Karen's direction. "I returned to Liverpool from Terezin, married Margaret, and resumed my medical career, studying to become an orthopaedic surgeon. I decided to specialise in paediatrics, and here I am in Whiston working with beautiful young patients like Karen." He smiled. Mr Strach's story moved me deeply and confirmed beyond doubt his status as a caring humanitarian.

Back in Mr Strach's office a few minutes later, he studied an x-ray of Karen's hips on a light box and pointed to it with his pen. "The heads of Karen's femora are in joint but are quite large, giving the impression of partial dislocation. This is nothing to be concerned about and is normal in the circumstances. She is doing remarkably well and is a credit to you both." Rita and I beamed. "Keep up the good work."

I lifted Karen off my lap and we prepared to leave. "Oh, I almost forgot," Mr Strach said. "Please call in at the appliance workshop on the way out. One of our technicians will measure Karen for her first wheelchair. She'll be going to school soon and we need to get her mobile."

-0-0-0-0-0-

On April 3, 1971, nearly two years after the wages robbery, and just a few months after most of the gang had been sentenced to long stretches in prison, we moved into a new house in the picturesque Cheshire village of Woolston. We drove there in my new car, a sporty two-tone Ford Anglia 105E saloon, with a rear windscreen angled back in the distinctive sweeping style of the classic Anglia marque.

Nine

Our brand-new semi-detached house at 62 Epping Drive was situated in an open-plan cul-de-sac in the village of Woolston, approximately twenty miles east of Liverpool and a thirty-minute drive to my workplace at United Biscuits. There was a sprawling garden to the rear and a smaller plot at the front, although when we moved in they were no more than rubble-strewn mud heaps. The house had a spacious lounge, a combined kitchen and dining room, three bedrooms and a bathroom. Walls and ceilings were painted in oyster-coloured emulsion and the floorboards were bare.

A lot of work lay ahead. I intended to lay carpets throughout the house, sow lawns in the front and back gardens, build a lean-to garage, and pave a driveway from the sidewalk to the garage doors. I also intended to install parallel steel bars to the side of the house so that Karen could practice her walking.

We had hired a van to haul our furniture from Hans Road and when we had finally moved the last crates and cartons into the house, we were absolutely knackered!

"I'm glad that's over, Rio. I never want to move house again," I said to my wife. We were sitting in the lounge sipping tea and Karen was in bed, finally asleep after an exciting day.

"It's done now, thank God. When do you think we'll be able to get the carpets?" Rita asked.

"We'll go into Warrington tomorrow and order them"

"We need a toilet roll holder, towel rail, light bulbs, and— "

"Make a list and we'll get them tomorrow from Warrington market." I was too tired to think. "Did you notice they have started work on the new school? It should be finished in the summer." Rita nodded as she struggled to read the Daily Mirror in the gloom.

The realisation it was almost dark reminded me we had no lights. "I'll just pop round to Irene's to borrow a few light bulbs until tomorrow. I won't be long." My sister, Irene, brother-in-law, Chris, and their three-month-old daughter, Jacqueline, lived a short walk away. I grabbed my navy-surplus donkey jacket and left the house.

Outside it was almost dark, yet at the top of the close a man toiled in his garden, wielding a spade. He saw me come out and waved me over. "Hello, mate," he said in a rural accent that marked him as a *woolly-back* to my urban ears. "How's it going. My name's Bob Bennett." He held out a mud-caked hand, which I reluctantly shook.

"Pleased to meet you, Bob. I'm Dave Verinder. We've just moved in and we've got no light bulbs." I shrugged a self-deprecatory smile.

"You won't get any this time of night. The Spar closes at seven."

"That's no problem. My sister lives five minutes away in Berkshire Drive, so I'm just off to borrow some."

"Hold on a sec", I've probably got some you can have."

"Please don't trouble yourself, Bob, I'm sure my sister will have some."

"It's no trouble. Just give me a minute." He slipped off his green Wellington boots at the door and went inside. Seconds later, he was back. "What are you standing out there for? Come on in." I followed him into his lounge. "This is my wife, Christine, and my daughter, Karen-Louise." A slim woman with short blonde hair, shaped in a bob, was sitting in an armchair reading a story to a little replica of herself. Karen-Louise was probably the same age as our Karen. I shook hands with Christine and smiled at Karen-Louise. "I'll just get the light bulbs," Bob said, disappearing into the kitchen.

"What a coincidence," I said to Christine. "I have a daughter named Karen, too. You'll probably meet her tomorrow. Maybe the girls would like to play together."

"That would be nice, wouldn't it Karen?" Karen-Louise smiled shyly.

Bob returned with a six-pack of 100-watt light bulbs and handed them to me.

"I'd better be going," I said. "My wife, Rita, is sitting in the dark trying to read the paper." They laughed. We were all a bit nervous meeting for the first time, but I was happy to have met the first of our neighbours and pleased they were friendly. I left Bob to pick up his spade and wellies from the driveway and walked back across the road to my house.

"That was quick," Rita said, as I took off my jacket.

"I didn't go to Irene's. I've just met our new neighbours, Bob and Christine. They gave me the light bulbs. They are really nice and have a daughter around Karen's age. Her name is Karen-Louise."

"Two Karens, huh? I hope they become friends." Rita stood up, stumbled, and clutched her midriff.

"Do you still have that pain?" I asked.

"It's nothing. It's probably indigestion." Rita had been suffering abdominal pain for the past few weeks.

"I'll register at the doctor's surgery in Dam Lane tomorrow and make an appointment for you."

Over the next few weeks, we straightened out the mess of boxes and crates and Rita set about making the house into a home. We shopped in Warrington Market for carpets and curtains and other bits and pieces, and soon we were settled into our little dream house. Karen and Karen-Louise became friends, and Bob and Christine were frequent visitors. I had two weeks leave from work and, learning that April was a good time for germination, I decided to get the lawns sown with a standard mixture of perennial rye grass and hardy meadow grass. I hired a rotavator and began the back-breaking task of turning over the huge areas of soil in the front and back gardens, piling the assorted rubble into a heap to use later as hard-core for the base of the garage. Raking fertilizer into the loose soil, scattering grass seed, and saturating the whole area with water was less arduous and more satisfying. Lines of string festooned with scraps of newspaper kept the birds away, and three weeks later the first green shoots were starting to sprout. A few more weeks and a glorious green carpet covered the front and back yards. I planted a miniature rose tree in the centre of the front lawn and the house now looked like the one illustrated in the original brochure.

During this period, Dave and Jane Roughley moved in next door. Dave was a burly rugby union scrum half who played for Liverpool and was just the kind of guy I needed to help me build a garage, which he was more than happy to do. We ordered the bricks through the site foreman, dug out the base, replacing the soil with hard-core rubble topped by a layer of ready-mixed concrete, and hired a professional brick-layer. A week later, my gleaming Ford Anglia had its own roof to protect it from the elements.

Rita's Dad, Sylvester, had some steel parallel bars made in work, and, laying down a few rows of flagstones to the side of the house, I hammered the legs of the bars into the ground to flank the paved area and soon Karen had her very own space to practice walking. Karen's made-to-measure wheelchair was delivered, and we looked forward to the new primary school being completed in good time for its scheduled opening in September. I was very pleased with life.

A few months earlier, I had been browsing through *Link* magazine, published by the Association for Spina Bifida and Hydrocephalus, when I came across an advertisement for a hand-propelled tricycle, specially designed for children such as Karen. It had a bench seat and back-rest between the rear wheels, and horizontal padded foot-rests. "Pedals", which could be turned by hand, were positioned where the handlebars would normally be. The "pedals" turned a chain attached to the front wheel by a fixed cog. By using hands only, the trike could be propelled and steered at the same time. As soon as I saw it, I understood the possibilities it would open up for Karen and had to buy one for her. The trikes were built to order and came in several sizes. I knew we would have some money spare after selling the house in Hans Road so I immediately placed an order.

We received the trike in plenty of time for Karen's fifth birthday. I had hidden it in the new garage. On the morning of her birthday, I carried Karen outside while Rita opened the garage door. Karen's eyes lit up the neighbourhood when she saw the sparkling powder-blue frame of the trike.

"Dad, is it really my bike?" she gasped.

"Yes, sweetheart, it's really your bike. Happy birthday!" I sat her on the bench seat and lifted her legs into the foot-rests. "All you have to do is turn the handles and you're on your way." She needed no further prompting, haring down the path and out into the road. I struggled to run alongside her as she whizzed down the cul-de-sac. It was then I realised I hadn't told her how to brake! I grabbed the back-rest. "Stop pedalling, Karen!" I shouted, dragging the trike to a halt. "I forgot to tell you how to stop. You need to "pedal" backwards to operate the brake." I showed her how to do it. "And stay on the sidewalk," I bellowed at her receding back as she flew down the street.

The new trike made an enormous difference to Karen's quality of life. For the first time she could keep up with her friends. I taught her the basics of the Highway Code and warned her never to cross a road without first looking right, left and right again. The unusual hand controls caused a bit of a stir in the neighbourhood. Everywhere Karen went on her trike, perhaps to the local Spar supermarket or to Irene's house in Berkshire Drive, people were amazed at this wonderful means of transport. Karen was now truly mobile. When she wasn't walking in her callipers, she used her new wheelchair around the house and her trike outdoors. I preferred to see her riding her trike than pushing herself around in the wheelchair. When she was on the trike, somehow, she appeared perfectly normal.

-0-0-0-0-0-

I tore open the brown envelope and opened the letter. It was headed "Warrington Borough Council, Education Department", and I began to read…

Dear Mr Verinder,

Thank you for the completed Preference Form in respect of your daughter, Karen. I regret to inform you that the new Woolston CE Aided Primary School will not be ready for occupation until September 1972, one year after Karen is due to begin her schooling.

We note Karen's special needs and would inform you that we have three special needs schools in the Warrington area, but none are suitable for children with physical disabilities. Also, existing primary schools in the area are unable to facilitate wheelchairs.

In the circumstances, we can offer you a private in-home tutor for three days per week, beginning Monday 6 September 1971.

I trust this meets with your approval.

Yours sincerely…

"Arsehole," I swore under my breath. "No, it doesn't meet with my approval!"

"What's the matter, love?" Rita asked. I had just returned from work, and we were in the kitchen. Rita was cooking dinner and Karen was upstairs in the bath.

"The new school won't be ready until next year and all they can offer Karen is a home tutor for three days a week! According to this…" I brandished the letter. "…they don't have any schools suitable for a child in a wheelchair. She can't be stuck at home; she has to mix with other kids. I'm not standing for this bullshit."

"But what can we do?" Rita asked.

"All it takes is a few ramps, a few hand rails in the toilet," I fumed. "I'm gonna write to our local MP… see what can be done. I'll write to the Director of Education, too. I'm not putting up with this crap." I prowled around the kitchen, madder than a Spanish bull tormented by picadors.

"Calm down, Dave," Rita urged. "Everything will work out fine, I'm sure."

"Everything won't work out fine unless we do something about it," I snapped. "While all the other kids are at school, Karen will be at home with some old spinster who's been put out to grass!"

"Stop shouting, for God's sake! Will a personal tutor be so bad? After all, Karen will get the complete attention of a qualified teacher."

I calmed down and thought on what Rita had said. "But what about mixing with other kids and making friends? She'll miss out on a lot by not going to school."

"If the school has no facilities for wheelchairs and no disabled toilets then Karen will struggle anyway. She'll be better off at home." Rita's voice was calm and reasonable.

"We can ask them to put in ramps and modify one of the toilets. It's not too much to ask, is it?"

"There's no harm in asking, I suppose."

"Then I'll write the letters tonight."

I pocketed the letter from the Council and climbed the stairs to the sound of splashing from the bathroom. "Time to wash your hair, sweetheart," I shouted to Karen.

As it turned out, I was to fight a long battle against the local Council trying to ensure my daughter received the same level of education as her able-bodied contemporaries. I wrote to the local Member of Parliament and to the Director of Education trying to force the authorities to build access ramps, widen doors, provide hand rails in toilets and generally conform to the prevailing law of the land relating to access. Unfortunately, the law applied only to new buildings and I was thwarted at every turn. For the time-being, I would have to accept the offer of home tutoring.

I was furious, but mostly with myself. We had moved to Woolston to be close to a suitable primary school, but I hadn't thought to check it would be built on time. A further irony was that a perfectly suitable special school, Sandfield Park, was situated just a few miles from where we used to live, but my pig-headed stubbornness refused to accept anything less than Karen attending a mainstream school. I was consoled by the knowledge that Woolston Church of England Primary would be ready next year, and it would be situated just a couple of hundred yards from our house. The new school would be a single-storey, state-of-the-art facility for up to 225 children aged from 5 to 11 years. I had seen the plans, and it would be perfect.

-0-0-0-0-0-

The 'phone on my Shift Manager's desk in United Biscuits' computer room rang and rang and rang. I was in the tape library preparing the next job to run on the new IBM System/360 Model 40 computer. "Will someone answer that bloody 'phone!" I shouted. Silence, except for the jarring sound of the telephone. I threw the magnetic tape I was holding onto a trolley and jogged over to my desk. *Where the hell was Tony Lane and that tosser, Brown?*

"Computer Room," I answered.

"Dave, it's Irene." *Why was my sister phoning me at work?* "There's no need to panic, but Rita's been taken to Warrington Infirmary by ambulance. She has a problem with her gall-bladder and needs an operation. Karen is here with me."

My heart fluttered and I glanced at my watch. It was half-past two, half an hour from the end of my shift. "Shit, I knew there was something wrong with her. I'll get someone to cover for me and head up to the hospital. I'll phone you from there." I slammed down the receiver. *Where the hell were Lane and Brown?*

I grabbed my jacket and headed through the bustling Punch Room to the canteen, oblivious to the throng of boisterous girls bashing out holes in cards for tonight's payroll data. Tony Lane and Keith Brown were sipping muddy coffee and gossiping. "What are you two doing in here?" I growled. They stared sheepishly into their plastic cups. "Never mind. Look, my wife's been rushed into hospital and I have to go. Tony, will you take over? Tonight's payroll is almost set to go. You just need the data from Mrs. Taylor." I ran out without waiting for a reply. They'd be fine. Tony was a good man.

Keith was competent, but crazy. A few weeks ago, on the night shift, I had been asleep in the canteen during my lunch break, which I had the dubious honour of sharing with Brown. Suddenly, the silence was shattered by a booming thunderclap and I fell off the row of straight-backed chairs that served as my bed. Grabbing the edge of a Formica-topped table, I pulled myself from the floor. A small plume of blue smoke hovered over the table and there was a scorch mark on one of its edges. A handful of live ammunition, yes… real bullets, was scattered over the table-top. A white-faced Brown still held the cigarette lighter he had used to heat up one of the rounds! We never did find that bullet but, at that moment, I wished it had been embedded in a tender part of Brown's anatomy.

My Ford Anglia almost flew back to Warrington. Leaving it in the hospital car park off Lovely Lane, I dashed up the old stone steps of the Victorian Infirmary into the Accident and Emergency department and enquired after my wife. She was having an operation to remove her gall-bladder and appendix, and I was told to wait. I sat and fretted for what seemed like hours. My thoughts strayed to the night, nine years earlier, when we had first met.

It was September 1962 and I was going out with a girl called Ann Small at the time. One night, when I knocked at Ann's door in Vulcan Street, Garston, her mother told me that she had gone to see one of her friends, Kay Williams, who lived in Canterbury Street, a short walk away.

I was singing softly to myself as I strolled up Canterbury Street… *Love, love me do… you know I love you… I'll always be true… so pleeeease…*

love me do... The Beatles were my favourite band. I knocked at number 110 and the door was opened by a slip of a girl with a mischievous grin and twinkling blue eyes. "What do you want?" she demanded.

"Is Ann Small here?"

"Ann! It's for you," she shouted back down the hall, remaining on the doorstep.

Ann came to the door, looking nervous and uncomfortable. "Rita, go back inside," she said. She waited until Rita had disappeared before delivering the good news. "Dave, I'm sorry but I don't want to see you anymore."

Shit! We had only been seeing each other for a few weeks, and I thought we were getting on well. "Why?" I asked.

"I've met someone else."

My lips twitched but there was nothing more to be said. She went back inside the house and closed the door in my face. I didn't know it then but I had just been dumped by my current girlfriend and met my future wife within a period of a few minutes.

I was interrupted from my daydream by a nurse. "Mr Verinder, your wife has had her operation and has been taken to the Women's Surgical Ward."

"How is she?"

"She's had a *cholecystectomy* and *appendectomy*, the surgical removal of the gall bladder and appendix. Don't worry, she'll be fine. You can go up to the ward now if you want." She directed me up the stairs.

Rita's bed was enclosed by screens and I found her sleeping off the anaesthetic. I sat on the edge of a visitor's chair holding her hand. She awoke for a moment, eyes fluttering, whispered something unintelligible, and was soon asleep once more.

After a while, the screens swished aside and a green-clad doctor with a mask hanging loosely around his neck introduced himself. I can't remember his name, but he looked like the Kenneth Williams character, Doctor Tinkle, in the *Carry On Doctor* movie, so let's call him Tinkle. "Mr Verinder, your wife was admitted with severe abdominal pain caused by gallstones," said Tinkle, flashing a toothy grin like a donkey contemplating a sack of carrots. "She needed surgery to remove her gall bladder and, while we were rummaging around, we noticed her appendix was inflamed, so we took that out as well."

"Will she be okay?"

"She'll be right as rain in no time at all. Neither the gall bladder nor the appendix is a vital organ and the body can cope perfectly well without them."

"I know the appendix is not essential but what about the gall bladder?" I asked.

"The gall bladder is a small sac which holds bile, a digestive juice produced by the liver and used to break down dietary fats." Tinkle was in his element. "Gallstones are a common disorder of the digestive system usually caused by the crystallisation of excess cholesterol in the bile.

Cholecystectomy, or surgical removal of the gall bladder, is therefore recommended if gallstones are causing problems. Your wife's stones were as big as cherries and blocking the bile ducts leading to the small intestines. Nasty little beggars, but we've got rid of them now."

"How long will she be in hospital?"

"Seven to ten days, I would think. We've made quite a large incision in her abdominal wall, which will take a little time to heal. We'll take the stitches out in about a week and review the situation then." We shook hands and he left.

Over the next few days, Rita was in severe pain, despite being prescribed strong analgesic tablets. On the fourth day following the surgery, a nurse changing Rita's dressing noticed that the wound was severely inflamed. Rita's abdomen was swollen as though she were pregnant. Tinkle was called and he immediately decided to cut into the wound without the benefit of a local anaesthetic, releasing a fountain of yellow pus and a piercing scream from the patient. A course of strong antibiotics completed the treatment, and slowly Rita began to get better.

The first time I saw her wound, the stitches had just been taken out. The seven-inch raw scar looked like a jagged zipper! The holes left by the sutures were at least an inch apart. Whoever was responsible didn't have a degree in embroidery, that's for sure. These were bloody great dog stitches! No matter, my wife was well again and we could get on with our lives.

Ten

Soon after Rita was discharged from hospital, we decided to spend the weekend in Anglesey to aid her recuperation. Through the ASBAH *Link* magazine, I had heard about a guest house, situated in the scenic harbour-town of Benllech, which could accommodate wheelchairs, and managed to make last-minute reservations.

Our route to North Wales along the A55 was littered with the ruins of ancient castles, some no more than a collection of disjointed dry-stone walls, others almost intact. From Bodelwydden, through Abergele, to Conwy I marvelled at these historical relics and wondered how, with the primitive tools of the day, the artisans had managed to build such monumental citadels, and all of them within a single century.

Hundreds of years later, modern tradesmen couldn't even build a primary school on time, let alone a castle, although the Welsh *were* being invaded, raped and pillaged at the time, which must have acted as a compelling incentive.

I steered my Ford Anglia off the A55 at Bangor and headed into the mountains. The panoramic view from the Llanberis road was intoxicating. High above the thirteenth century town of Caernarfon, as the sunlight danced against the castle walls, we could see the swiftly flowing waters of the Menai Strait, which separated the majestic mountains of Snowdonia from the rolling meadows of the Isle of Anglesey.

The Llanberis Road led directly into Caernarfon town, and within a few minutes we had passed through a rough archway in the castle wall and stopped outside a paved beer garden in front of the *Black Boy Inn*.

"This looks like a nice place to stop for lunch, Rio," I said. "What d'you think?"

"It looks great. We can sit outside and eat our sandwiches."

I unfolded Karen's wheelchair from the boot, lifted her from the car and placed her gently onto the cushioned seat. "Don't go far, Karen. I'm just going into the pub to get some drinks. I won't be long."

Ducking through the low door-frame, I inhaled the musky scent of local wild flowers which overflowed from the hanging baskets beside the entrance. I crossed to the bar, and ordered a pint of bitter, a half of shandy, and a glass of lemonade. The landlady was immaculate in a black dress, with a high collar and zipped front, which resembled a Mary Quant "Banana Split" design.

As she busied herself with my order, I glanced at the photographs hanging from a stout oak column which formed a corner of the bar. My eye was drawn to a picture of a Royal Welch Fusilier in traditional dress uniform, red coat, resplendent with white piping, epaulettes and silver buttons, black trousers with a broad red stripe down each side, polished black boots, and the crowning glory—a bearskin hat with white feathers. Beside the Fusilier stood the regimental Kashmir goat, smiling through his beard. He looked just like my boss at United Biscuits. The goat, that is, not the soldier.

I heard the clinking of glasses and turned back to the bar. "There you are, my dear, that'll be thirty-five pence, please," the landlady said with a soft Welsh lilt. I automatically calculated how much that was in old money—seven shillings—and handed over the newly-minted coins. Decimalisation of the currency had been implemented in February and I still wasn't used to it.

I carried the drinks outside and found Rita sitting on a bench at a heavy oak table, admiring the view of Caernarfon Castle. Karen, who had been inspecting souvenirs through the window of a gift shop, saw me come out of the bar and hared down the cobbles in her wheelchair, almost loosening her teeth in the process. She approached me at a lick and spread her arms. "Look, Dad, no hands!" She grabbed the wheels and came to an abrupt halt, inches from spreading me and the tray of drinks all over the beer garden.

"You little madam," I grinned. "You'll do me an injury one day."

Karen had become an expert wheelchair handler in just a few months, although I had mixed feelings about it. Like the ubiquitous callipers and walking frame, the wheelchair seemed to emphasise Karen's disability. When she was speeding around on her hand-propelled trike she seemed free, like a bird released from its cage. When she was in her wheelchair, she seemed restricted, somehow. I was beginning to realise what a lifetime of disability would mean to my daughter.

I shoved the negative thoughts to that part of my mind reserved for the future, and we enjoyed our lunch in the August sunshine to the cries of seagulls and the smell of fish and seaweed from the harbour.

Back in the car, we headed for the Britannia Bridge which would take us over the Menai Strait to *Ynys Mon*, the Isle of Anglesey, and the town of Benllech, which nestled against the craggy coastline west of Red Wharf Bay. I had memorised the route from my RAC Road Atlas—a straight run down the A5025 coast road, passing close to the village of Llanfairpwllgwyngyllgogerychwyrndrobwllllantysiliogogogoch, which in Welsh, I told Karen, translated to "St Mary's Church, in the Hollow of the White Hazel, near a Rapid Whirlpool and the Church of St. Tysilio, near the Red Cave". As we passed by, we searched for a white hazel near a whirlpool without success. We saw plenty of churches, but there was no red cave to be found either.

By mid-afternoon we had arrived at the *Benllech Isaf* guest house, a converted Edwardian beach residence. Situated at the western tip of Benllech beach on a rocky headland washed by foaming waves, *Benllech Isaf* was both picturesque and functional. Our ground-floor room was warmly furnished in traditional Welsh style, with lots of polished wood and lacy fabrics, a standard double bed, a stow-able put-up bed for Karen, and plenty of room to manoeuvre the wheelchair.

From our bedroom window, looking out over Red Wharf Bay, we had the most wonderful view of Puffin Island against the stunning backdrop of the Snowdonian mountains on the mainland. As I gazed out of the window at *Benllech Isaf*, with Karen balanced on my lap, a lonely Atlantic Puffin, with corpulent white breast, curved amber bill, and golden apricot webs for feet, headed home to roost.

The Benllech weekend proved to be enjoyable in so many ways. Besides Rita being able to relax and recover from her surgery, Karen learned a lot about nature and geography, more than she could ever learn in school, or from a home-tutor. Experiencing at first hand the wonders of the natural world was so stimulating to her young mind.

And she got to drive the car. Well, not drive exactly. She sat on my knee and steered the Anglia down a private road to the beach at Moelfre. Not many five-year-olds got to do that.

-0-0-0-0-0-

The first time I met Joanna Parkes, I realised I may have been hasty in my deprecatory opinion of home-tutors. She was no old, grazing spinster. She was twenty-five, vivacious, witty, committed and, most of all, she bonded with Karen faster than a tube of Bostik.

Joanna came to our house in Epping Drive each Monday, Wednesday and Friday during the normal school term, from ten o'clock to three o'clock. She gave Karen quality time, improving her reading and writing beyond measure. The hours of schooling were shorter, but the one-on-one approach was of enormous benefit to Karen.

There was also plenty of time for walking practice without working Karen too hard. The parallel bars, installed at the side of the house, were invaluable. Karen had developed tremendous upper-body strength which enabled her to negotiate stairs. We helped her develop an unusual, but effective, technique. Karen would sit on a step and push down on her hands to ease her bottom up and over the riser onto the next level, and so on to the top.

She still needed help to get onto the toilet, but she could manage most other everyday tasks. The only thing missing was speed. Everything was accomplished in slow motion.

During that first Autumn term, Joanna became a member of the family. She worked hard with Karen and there was no evidence Karen was falling behind her contemporaries. If anything, she was ahead, especially with her reading. I began to realise that Karen might actually benefit from this combination of close tuition and development of her walking technique. She also needed help from a carer from time to time. Rita provided this support while Karen was being educated at home, but who would provide it at Woolston Church of England Primary School?

On impulse, I decided to visit Sandfield Park School in Liverpool. On the way into work at United Biscuits for an afternoon shift, I made a short detour and headed up the long driveway at Sandfield Park into the car park. Several special ambulances and Sunshine coaches, with hydraulic wheelchair lifts on the back, were patiently waiting for the end of the school day. Next to the car park was a small paved playground and sports field.

I felt like a burglar as I crept around the outside of the school, peering into classrooms. The scenes resembled conventional classrooms, except various walking aids were scattered about and some children were sitting at their desks in wheelchairs. The number of children in each class was small, perhaps ten or twelve, and there was a teacher with one or two assistants or carers helping with the children's physical needs, which ranged from help with holding a pen for cerebral palsy sufferers to simply moving objects out of the way for those walking with frames or callipers.

I was impressed.

-0-0-0-0-0-

"Dave McGuiness wants to see you." Paddy Tighe, the Computer Operations Manager at United Biscuits, had called me into his office. Dave was the Systems Development Manager and I had an idea what he wanted to talk to me about. A friend of mine, George Irving, was head of the systems programming team and he had been bugging me for months to join him "upstairs" as a Trainee Programmer. At that time, I was a shift manager in the operations department and I received a handsome premium on my salary for working shifts. I hated the shifts but loved the money.

"What does he want?"

"He wants to offer you a job. I told him he was wasting his time, but you can talk to him if you want." Paddy had a beguiling Irish accent and the irritating habit of assuming he knew what was best for his "boys". I was loyal to Paddy, though, and to his deputy, Keith Faulkner, who had lured me to United Biscuits in the first place.

I knocked on McGuiness's door and stepped inside. He was wading through a pile of expense receipts with the expression of a condemned man sucking a lemon. His face brightened as he looked up. "Dave, come in... shut the door... sit." McGuiness was direct but, reputedly, a caring, supportive boss.

"Paddy Tighe said you wanted to see me," I ventured.

"Yeah, how do you fancy working for me?"

"As a programmer?"

"A trainee."

"I'm a shift manager now and Paddy says I have a big future in operations. Why would I want to take a step down?"

"You'll take a step down but, if my judgement is correct, you'll soon make up lost ground."

"What about wages?"

"You'll stay on the same money."

"With the shift allowance included?"

"No, but if you do well I'll make up your money later."

"Can I think about it?"

Without answering, he picked up his phone and punched in a number. "George, do you have a minute?"

A few moments later, George Irving navigated his bulky frame into the office. "George, tell this clown he'll be throwing away the best opportunity of his life if he doesn't join our team."

The sales spiel lasted thirty minutes. They worked me over like Joe Friday and his sidekick, Frank Smith, in a Dragnet episode. I didn't stand a chance. Three weeks later, at the beginning of May 1972, I joined the programming team.

-0-0-0-0-0-

Even though the new Woolston Church of England Primary School was almost complete, my unauthorised visit to Sandfield Park School had made up my mind. And when I told Rita, she was in favour too. Karen was going to be educated at Sandfield Park. Unfortunately, this meant moving house. Karen and Karen-Louise had become great mates, our neighbours were friendly, and we were settled, but we had to move. I had put an enormous amount of work into 62 Epping Drive, which meant we could sell at, if not a handsome, a fairly good-looking profit.

Irene, Chris and Jacqueline had left Woolston six months earlier and had settled near to Mum and Dad in Allerton, which made it easier for us to move back to Liverpool.

So, in July, a little over a year after moving to Woolston, we swapped rural contentment for urban bliss in West Derby, a leafy district of Liverpool, where my Uncle Harold lived. The house at 26 Parkside Drive, walking distance from Sandfield Park School, was a 1930's semi-detached property, in need of some decoration, but structurally sound. It had a sunken air-raid shelter in the back garden, which the estate agent forgot to mention, but which offered a handy place for me to hide during Rita's monthly bouts of PMT.

We'd hardly had time to unpack before we were off on a caravan holiday to Chwilog, near Pwllheli, in North Wales. Black Rock Sands, a picture-postcard stretch of beach between Criccieth and Porthmadog, was just a short drive away. For the first time, we were holidaying with Rita's family. Rita's Mum and Dad were sharing a caravan with her eldest sister, Betty, husband Bob, and children, Julie and Robbie. Rita's Auntie Nina and Uncle John, cousin Ann and husband Ray also had a caravan on the same site.

With Karen thriving, Rita and I decided it was time to add to our family. We found plenty of time to be alone and the caravan's springs were tested to their limit during the following two weeks.

Soon after our return from North Wales, we were delighted to learn my sister, Irene, had given birth to a gorgeous curly-haired girl, Helen, who was born with all fingers, toes and faculties intact on August 16, the same day the Royal Moroccan Air Force fired upon King Hassan's plane during an attempted coup d'état. The missiles missed their target, but Helen was a big hit in our expanding family.

We now looked forward to Karen starting school, and on Monday, 4 September, 1972, the day finally arrived. We drove to Sandfield Park and met Mrs. Fairhurst, the headmistress, who showed us around and introduced us to the deputy-head, Mr Cox, and Karen's teacher, Mrs. Blundell. Karen pushed herself in her wheelchair and her wide smile proved we had made the right decision about her schooling. We also learned that Mr Strach would continue to monitor Karen's walking development during his regular visits to Sandfield Park. Karen had recently been fitted with new thigh-length callipers, which were lighter and easier to manoeuvre, but had no back support. She was a little wobbly with these callipers but Mr Strach assured us she would soon be able to cope and, as usual, he was right.

Before we left Karen in Mrs. Blundell's capable hands, Mrs. Fairhurst arranged for Karen's transport to and from school via one of the schools converted ambulances. A truly momentous day was capped by Rita's whispered announcement as we travelled back to Parkside Drive in our Ford Anglia. She was pregnant!

I considered Chwilog for the baby's name, but not for long.

-0-0-0-0-0-

"Knock, knock," I said.

"Who's there?" replied Karen.

"Alpaca."

"Alpaca who?"

"Alpaca the suitcases and you packa the bags!"

It was Boxing Day and the Verinder clan was enjoying cold turkey sandwiches at my sister, Irene's, house in Allerton. Irene, Chris, Jacqueline and baby, Helen, were joined by Mum and Dad, my younger brothers, Geoffrey and Barry, and sister Jean, as well as myself, Rita and Karen. Jean was now sixteen-years-old, Geoff fourteen and Barry would be thirteen on New Year's Eve. Mum and Dad had enjoyed a ten-year rest between Irene and Jean.

Rita sat with a plate balanced on her expanding midriff, eating for two.

Shining with vitality, Karen's long, golden hair was braided and ribboned. She wore a white dress with red polka-dots as big as old pennies, the epitome of enchanting, radiant girlhood.

"Your turn Karen," I said.

She thought for a moment, her arms draped over the wheelchair. "Knock, knock."

"Who's there?"

"Thea."

"Thea who?"

"Thea later, alligator."

We all laughed, except for Geoff and Barry, who were watching a *Carry On* film on television.

Jacqui, who was balanced on the footrests of Karens wheelchair and trying to climb onto her lap, slipped and fell in a heap on the carpet, knocking off one of Karen's shoes in the process. Jacqui picked herself up and toddled off to annoy someone else. As Karen reached down to pick up her shoe—a difficult manoeuvre whilst sitting in her wheelchair, but not impossible—Mum started to get up off the couch. "I'll get your shoe for you, Karen," she said.

"It's okay, Mum," I intervened, sipping on my vodka and tonic. "She can manage."

Mum ignored me and reached for the shoe.

"Mum, don't!" I snapped.

She took a half-step back, shocked by my outburst. I had never before raised my voice to my mother.

"What's the matter with you," Mum yelled. "You can see she's struggling."

"Mum, please let her do it herself," I said firmly, but a little less aggressively. "She can reach it."

Karen's lips quivered, signalling the onset of tears. She hated confrontation. A stern look in her direction was usually enough to open the floodgates.

"I'm only trying to help!" Mum bristled.

"I know," I said, "but you're not really helping at all. What happens next time her shoe falls off and you're not there to pick it up?"

Mum glared at me, continuing the argument with her eyes.

With silent rivers streaming down her face, Karen retrieved her shoe and strained to slip it over her foot. Rita pulled herself up from her chair and put her arm around Karen's shoulders, but she didn't try to help with the shoe.

"You're too bloody hard on her." Mum was like a Jack Russell snapping around my ankles. "Where's the harm in helping her now and then."

"I know you mean well, but Karen hasn't come this far by us doing everything for her. That's the easy way out. D'you think I like to see her struggle?" I was getting irritated, even a little emotional. Maybe it was the vodka.

Nobody else was keen to get into this debate. I expected Dad to intervene on Mum's side, but he kept his jaws firmly clamped. Rita seemed embarrassed and implored me with her eyes to end the argument.

Mum was from an Edge Hill family known as the *Fightin' McCormicks* and wouldn't let it go so easily. "She has a hard-enough time as it is without you making it worse," she hissed.

"I'm not making it worse!" I was getting up a head of steam, too. "You haven't got a clue what it's like. You only see her for a few hours at weekends. I see her struggle all the time, so don't tell me I'm making it worse for her. I'm trying to give her independence for God's sake!"

Mum glowered over her glasses and was about to say something else when Dad gave her a sharp nudge in the ribs. She sprang to her feet with the agility of a Welsh mountain goat, storming out of the lounge and into the kitchen. For several moments, the silence was punctuated only by the familiar voices of Sid James and Barbara Windsor as they cavorted around the television screen.

"Dave, go and apologise to your mother," Rita whispered.

"Apologise?" I was almost apoplectic. "I've done nothing to apologise for." I gulped down the last of my vodka, set the glass down on the floor, and folded my arms in a gesture of defiance.

I stewed for a while. I had never rowed with my Mum before. She had given me plenty of verbal lashings when I was young, but I had never dared to answer her back. This time, though, I knew I was right. Or was I? Maybe we were both right. It was Boxing Day, after all; the season of good will. Perhaps I *was* too tough on Karen? No, to hell with it. The proof was sitting in front of me. Karen had overcome her difficulties to become a sparkling, determined six-year-old. I was proud of her and loved her beyond measure. I shouldn't have made such a big issue of this incident, though.

When I entered the kitchen, Mum had her back to me and was washing the dishes. I put my arms around her from behind and kissed her on the cheek, which was glistening with tears. "I'm sorry for upsetting you, Mum," I said.

She leaned back against me, sighed, but didn't speak.

"I have this dream," I said. "In this dream, I see Karen married with children, twins, a boy and a girl; I see her cooking the family meal in her own kitchen; I see her changing her babies' nappies, bathing and feeding them; I see her vacuuming carpets and polishing windows; I see her shopping in Tesco's. Sometimes, when I see her doing these things, she's in a wheelchair, sometimes, miraculously, she's walking. I don't know what the future holds, but I'm going to make sure Karen has the best chance possible of a normal life. If I have to be tough on her, then I will be tough. But not too tough."

Mum turned and flung her hands around my neck. She hugged me tightly, leaned away, then rubbed frothy Fairy suds onto my cheeks, before disappearing, laughing, back into the lounge.

Eleven

An urgent poke in the ribs brought me awake in an instant. My first thought was I had wet the bed, and I hadn't done that for more than twenty-five years. "Dave, the baby's coming, my water has broken!"

"Don't panic," I soothed. "I'll call an ambulance." I dived out of bed, fumbled around for my jeans, and began to pull them on while hopping towards the bedroom door. I reached down and carefully zipped over my nakedness, thumped down the stairs, picked up the 'phone, and dialled nine-nine-nine. Thankfully, Karen was having a sleep-over with her Nan and Grandad Verinder.

The ambulance arrived a few minutes later, by which time I had pulled on a crew-necked sweater and helped Rita out of bed and into her housecoat. The ambulance crew strapped my bloated wife into a narrow aisle-chair and lugged her down the stairs, while I traipsed behind clutching her plastic wash bag. "Don't forget my make-up!" Rita yelled in between gasps. I ran back, tripping over the top stair, and rummaged around her dressing table like a wild boar hunting for truffles.

I found the makeup bag on the ottoman at the bottom of the bed, next to the towels she had left out a few nights earlier. I snatched up the lumpy velvet bag, crammed the towels under my arm, and raced down the stairs. I locked the front door, ran down the path, and climbed into the ambulance just before the doors were slammed shut. Rita was propped up on a trolley, arms around her bulging midriff, but she appeared calm between her one-per-minute contractions.

A little under ten minutes later, the ambulance pulled up outside Fazackerley Hospital's Maternity Unit. Rita waddled through the automatic doors, a paramedic holding each of her arms, and was ushered into the delivery suite by a clucking midwife. I was directed to a waiting room to take my place amongst a clutch of nervous fathers-to-be, some of whom, I learned, had been waiting through the night.

I retrieved a tattered copy of the *Liverpool Echo* from a stack of magazines, barely visible amongst the clutter of cigarette packets, chocolate-bar wrappers, and heaped ashtrays, and sat down on a padded bench seat. I turned to the sports page at the back of the paper. The dateline was Wednesday 18 April 1973, two days ago. Liverpool had beaten Coventry City 2-0 on the Tuesday night and the mighty Reds were about to be crowned champions of England for the umpteenth time. I read the same paragraph over and over.

Fifteen minutes later, a blue-uniformed staff nurse popped her head round the door of the waiting room and beckoned me to follow. My sphincter twitched uncontrollably as I bolted off the seat. When I caught up, she turned her head, her starched nurse's cap tilted at a coquettish angle.

"Your wife has had the baby," she said with a smile.

What? Already? It can't be! "Is everything OK?"

"Just follow me and you will see for yourself," she replied.

The nurse stopped at the door of a private side ward. "Come inside and meet your baby son," she said, opening the door with a flourish and standing aside. "Don't worry, he's just perfect!" she whispered as I passed by.

Rita's face was mottled from her recent exertions but she looked beatific as she held the wrinkled little bundle close to her breast, kissing his forehead before handing him to me. His face was stained with blood but he was the most beautiful baby boy I had ever seen. I cradled him in my arms, my vision blurred by tears of joy.

I peered into his midnight-blue eyes and whispered, "Welcome to the world, Michael David Verinder." I looked at Rita and my heart soared. How we had prayed that our baby would be healthy, and this time someone had been listening! I cherished the moment and locked it into my heart.

A plump Irish midwife reached out to take my son. "Sure, he looks just like his father," she said. "Will yer look at his eyes, now; they are beautiful, just beautiful! Let's get you cleaned up."

I took this as my cue to leave. Michael squealed as the midwife began to sponge him down. I kissed my radiant wife goodbye, promising to be back for the afternoon visit along with our daughter. I backed out of the delivery room waving and blowing kisses, certain my huge grin would have to be surgically removed!

As I strolled down the deserted hospital corridor, my thoughts lingered on my darling daughter, Karen, and I contemplated the circumstances of *her* birth, almost seven years earlier. The contrast was stark—a gaping chasm of disparate emotions. Today, I was jubilant; then, there had been only the darkest despair. Today, I was filled with hope; then, a dreadful sense of foreboding was my constant companion. How we got through that terrible time, I cannot say. I only know this—Rita and I have never seen our severely disabled daughter as a heavy burden, to be carried on sagging shoulders. Rather, we have accepted her as a precious gift, to be savoured and nurtured with love. And today she has a baby brother!

-0-0-0-0-0-

I bumped Karen's wheelchair through the double swing-doors of the maternity ward and, walking slowly down the aisle, looked left and right, searching for my wife and son amongst the other mothers and babies.

Karen had been staying with Mum and Dad for the past few days and, on the way to the hospital in my new Datsun Cherry hatchback, she had been bubbling with excitement. "Tell me again what he's like, Dad!"

"You'll see him in a few minutes."

"Oh, Dad, please!"

"Well, he's 20 inches long, weighs seven pounds and ten ounces, which is about the same as four bags of sugar, and he has auburn hair and blue eyes, just like you."

"Will I be able to hold him, Dad?"

"Of course you will, sweetheart. You'll be the first to hold him, just like I promised."

Karen spotted her Mum first. Rita was sitting in a high-backed chair next to a hospital bed, on the opposite side to the baby's moulded plastic crib, and she was bottle-feeding him.

"Mum! Mum! We're here!" Karen waved.

Rita's face shone with happiness. She stopped feeding the baby and his tiny lips puckered, searching for the nipple on the teat. Turning sideways so our daughter could see him face-on, Rita said, "What do you think of your baby brother, Karen?"

"He's gorgeous, Mum! Can I hold him, please?"

Rita stood and handed over the baby, ensuring Karen supported his head properly in the crook of her arm. "Would you like to feed him?" Rita asked.

"Can I... really?"

"Of course you can, honey-bunch. Here, take the bottle and tilt it like this. Just make sure there's always milk in the teat and he will do the rest."

Rita and I sat on the edge of the bed, watching our children, who were together for the first time. If there had ever been a happier day in my life, I couldn't remember it.

Karen's physical progress at Sandfield Park in her first year was extraordinary. She became more confident walking with her callipers and was able to perform most routine tasks, like going to the toilet, and more difficult tasks, like negotiating small steps, with little or no help from the in-class carers. She quickly formed a strong bond with her teacher, Mrs Blundell, and she integrated seamlessly into school life. Even as a six-year-old, her favourite pastime was chatting with the adults – teachers and carers alike – during breaks in the relaxed teaching regimen, and she was so happy in this environment that Rita and I didn't regret for a second our decision to send her there.

A typical day for Karen at Sandfield Park started at around 08:30, when she boarded her school "bus", which was in fact a Sunshine Coach with a tail lift for easy wheelchair boarding. The bus was provided by the Variety Children's Charity, which is devoted to the transportation and mobility of young disabled children and was founded by a group of Variety Club showbusiness personalities. The bus picked up a number of other disabled children living in the area and she would arrive at school at around 09:15. She would then take part in normal school lessons and activities, punctuated by breaks when her physical welfare was addressed with walking practice (using her recently-acquired elbow crutches), physiotherapy, and regular visits by Mr Strach, who closely monitored her progress. At around 15:30, she would board the bus for the journey home, arriving between 16:00 and 16:15.

Karen was also growing and pretty soon her precious tricycle was becoming a little small and she needed a new one, which we scrimped and saved to buy. I can't stress enough how much this meant to her quality of life. When not at school and, weather permitting, she would be outside on her trike playing with her new neighbourhood friends, most often with a near neighbour of her own age, Carol Stewart.

Karen's first year at Sandfield Park also coincided with a royal visit, when King Constantine and Queen Anne-Marie of Greece made a brief appearance at the school. Karen was particularly taken with the glamorous Anne-Marie, who was an ex-Danish princess and with whom she had her photograph taken.

-0-0-0-0-0-

When I left for work on a misty morning in November 1973, Karen was not feeling very well and Rita decided not to send her to school. By the time I returned around ten hours later, Karen was suffering severe headaches and bouts of dizziness, and she was running a temperature. With our daughter lolling on her lap, Rita pressed the rubber non-return valve which lay just under the skin behind Karen's right ear and said, "I am sure her shunt is blocked. Look how slowly the valve is coming back up."

Suddenly, Karen convulsed in Rita's arms and her eyes almost disappeared into the top of her skull. The convulsion probably lasted no more than 30 seconds but it seemed like an eternity before her body relaxed and she was responsive again.

"My head hurts, Dad", she moaned.

"I know sweetheart and we are going to make you better very soon." I turned to Rita, "I agree that it's most probably her valve. Let's get her checked out at Alder Hey." Fortunately, our six-month-old son had recently been fed and was sound asleep in his carry-cot. Rita whisked him off to Margaret Stewart, Carol's Mum and a trusted friend and neighbour, so that we could make the familiar dash to Alder Hey. During the short journey, Karen convulsed twice more in her mum's arms and Rita was alternately crying and trying to comfort our stricken daughter.

Our amateur diagnosis of a malfunctioning shunt was quickly confirmed and Karen was prepped for emergency surgery. Two hours later, in the Neurological ward, Karen was sleeping off the anaesthetic. Her head was swathed in bandages. "I hope they haven't shaved off her beautiful hair," Rita whimpered. A young, green-scrubbed surgeon, whose name I can't remember, joined us at Karen's bedside. "H...how did it go, doctor," I asked.

"The catheter carrying the cerebral fluid to Karen's bloodstream was severely degraded and, in fact, because Karen has grown considerably since it was installed, it was much too short and a complete replacement of both the shunt valve and the catheter was required. The operation went very well and Karen should suffer no harmful after-effects." He smiled encouragement.

"We were absolutely terrified when Karen was convulsing. We thought she was…". I choked up and couldn't finish.

"This is a common symptom of a blocked shunt and, if not treated urgently, it can result in brain damage. I understand how stressful this must have been for you, but you did the right thing by immediately bringing her to us and not waiting for an ambulance. She is going to be just fine so try not to worry."

Rita asked, "Have you shaved off her hair?"

"Well, of course, we had to shave off some hair, but the bare patch will be covered by her lovely long locks, so it won't be noticeable." Rita smiled for the first time.

The surgeon left us and, with Karen continuing to sleep soundly, we left her in the very capable hands of the wonderful Alder Hey nursing staff. Once again, we were heavily in their debt.

We arrived home around 11pm, tired and hungry, and picked up our baby son from our caring neighbours, Margaret and Peter Stewart. Thankfully, Karen was soon back to her bubbly self and the episode soon became a distant memory.

Soon after Karen's 8th birthday, she joined the Liverpool Challenge Club, a sports club for disabled youngsters, which encourages them to swim, take part in wheelchair races, and play games such as basketball and table tennis. She had good upper-body strength and could build up a fair head of steam in her wheelchair.

In October of 1974, the National Junior Games, organised by the British Sports Association for the Disabled, were due to take place in the grounds of Stoke Mandeville hospital, internationally renowned for rehabilitating quadriplegics and supported by the radio and television presenter, Jimmy Savile.

The Stoke Mandeville Sports Stadium for the Paralysed and other Disabled was the first of its type in the world and was formally opened in September 1969 by Queen Elizabeth II. The new stadium included a main sports hall with spectator's gallery, for sports such as basketball, fencing, weightlifting, and badminton, a 25-metre swimming pool with spectator's balcony, a two lane 10-pin bowling alley, a snooker room, an outdoor sports track with a sports field for javelin, shot putt, and archery, an indoor bowling green (upon which the famous air ace and amputee, Group Captain Douglas Bader, bowled the first wood), a table tennis hall, and bar. There was also a two-storey accommodation block at the rear of the stadium with downstairs dormitories for wheelchair users.

The children of the Liverpool Challenge Club were delighted to learn that they would be participating in the games and Karen was determined to take part in the wheelchair and swimming races and table tennis competition.

The Challenge Club was not wealthy and relied on parents to ferry the children to sports events. So, on the Friday afternoon before the games were due to start, Karen, Rita, Michael, and I duly arrived at the Stoke Mandeville stadium and were immediately impressed by the distinctive plaque at its entrance, consisting of three intertwined wheels bearing the motto FRIENDSHIP, UNITY, SPORTSMANSHIP.

The games were a great success and Karen managed to win two silver medals in the swimming and wheelchair races and a gold medal in the table tennis competition. It was heart-warming to see so many children overcome their disabilities to take part in the wide range of sports and the occasion left a lasting impression on our young family.

Our sentiments were echoed by the founder of the National Spinal Injuries Centre at Stoke Mandeville, Sir Ludwig Guttmann, who famously remarked, "If I ever did one good thing in my medical career, it was to introduce sport into the treatment and rehabilitation programme of spinal cord injury sufferers and other severely disabled." Thank you, Sir Ludwig!

Twelve

Mr Strach, Consultant Orthopaedic Surgeon, had finished examining Karen on a scheduled visit to Whiston Hospital towards the end of April, 1975. "I'm concerned about Karen's spine," he said.

Karen, almost nine years old now, had earlier demonstrated her ability to walk with leg callipers and elbow crutches. Her prowess had been gained through hours of daily exercise; sometimes she would practice climbing on and off steps, and other times she would attempt to walk backwards while opening a door, a particularly difficult manoeuvre.

"What are you concerned about?" I steadied my voice, mindful of Karen's presence. Rita was at home with our two-year-old son, Michael, who had enriched our lives beyond measure. It seemed we were destined for a life of highs and lows with nothing in between.

"We'll take some x-rays to confirm my diagnosis, but I'm afraid her spine has started to curve laterally into a sort of S-bend. Everyone's spine has a natural outward curve at the shoulders and an inward curve at the lower back, but Karen's spine is starting to bend sideways in a condition known as scoliosis."

Mr Strach handed me an x-ray request form and we left his office. Karen pushed herself to Radiology in her wheelchair. I stood on the rear foot levers and hitched a ride. Looking down, I saw her brow was furrowed. "Don't worry, sweetie, it's only an x-ray. No injections today, I promise."

Karen tilted her head back and gave me her most endearing gap-toothed smile. She wore her favourite red dress, and her long auburn hair was tied back in a ponytail. She had a long memory as far as needles were concerned after a number of spinal taps and countless other procedures, which associated syringes with intense pain.

In a green-curtained cubicle, I helped Karen undress, tied her into an oversized white gown, and wheeled her into the radiology room. I lifted her out of her wheelchair and laid her face-down on the glossy surface of the x-ray table.

A few minutes later, I reversed the procedure and, with Karen dressed and back in her wheelchair, we waited for the pictures to be developed. On the way back to Mr Strach, holding a large manila envelope, I couldn't resist a peek at the negatives. I cursed my curiosity.

Viewed on the light-box in Mr Strach's office, the S-shaped curvature appeared even more pronounced. Karen read her BBC TV Wombles annual. Mr Strach stroked his chin. "Some of the vertebrae have started to rotate, probably due to an imbalance in the muscles supporting the spine." He traced the outline of Karen's spine with his pen. "There are two lateral structural curves forming a classic scoliotic S-shape."

"What can you do about it?" I expected Mr Strach to wave his wand.

He thought for a moment. "I'm going to refer you to Mr Owen at Alder Hey Children's Hospital. He specialises in scoliosis of the spine and has had a lot of success with corrective surgery."

"She'll have to have surgery?"

"I'm afraid so. Once scoliosis begins it inevitably deteriorates. At the moment, the curvature is barely noticeable except on an x-ray, but over time it will become more pronounced, until it reaches the point where the internal organs become restricted, then crushed, and then. . ."

"Dad, look at Uncle Bulgaria. Isn't he funny?"

"Not now, sweetheart. Daddy's busy." I stroked her shiny ponytail.

As the impact of Mr Strach's words registered, my breathing became tight and shallow. I reached into my pocket for my Ventolin inhaler and took a couple of blasts. *Breathe slow and easy, calm yourself. . .* The salbutamol worked its magic and my breathing eased.

"Uncle Bulgaria's chasing Wellington, Dad. Look!" Karen pulled at my sleeve.

"Yes, love, he's very funny," I wheezed.

"Mr Verinder, are you alright?" Mr Strach peered over his horn-rimmed glasses.

"I'll be fine. . . Asthma. . . My mother's genes."

"Please, try not to worry. Mr Owen will look after Karen just fine. I'll write to him today and make an appointment for you to see him. It's unlikely surgery will be required for some years, but I'd like Mr Owen to review

Karen's case notes, look at the x-rays, and decide on a course of action."

-0-0-0-0-0-

A few months later, still waiting for confirmation of her appointment with Mr Owen, Karen brought a letter home from her headmaster at Sandfield Park School. I opened it expecting notification of an open day or field trip but found instead an invitation to attend a lecture at Alder Hey on the treatment of scoliosis. The lecturer was to be Robert Owen. I made a mental note to mark the date in my diary.

One evening in late June, as Rita and I took our seats in the lecture theatre at Alder Hey, we recognised and waved to several parents of Karen's school friends. Tommy and Eileen Ainscough were there, as were Peter and Margaret Jervis. Both families had children with spina-bifida. The room buzzed with conversation. On a small stage at the front stood a screen and a slide projector. After a few minutes, the lights dimmed and a formidable woman, the hospital matron, stout and imperious, vacated her seat in the front row, turned, and faced the audience. "Ladies and Gentlemen, please welcome Mr Robert Owen."

Polite applause swirled around the room as a man in his early forties stepped onto the stage and stood behind a lectern. Mr Owen was tall, slim, and balding, with small, round spectacles perched on his nose in a way that made him look over his glasses rather than through them. "Good evening, everyone, and thank you for coming." He spoke with a light Welsh accent.

He pressed a button on the slide projector and a powerful white beam lit up the screen with an image of a child lying on a special surgical bed. It was a wide shot, but I could see the child's head had a sort of band around it.

"This is a Stryker Bed, which I use to treat scoliosis of the spine. By applying positive pressure to the patient's skull and legs, the skeleton is stretched by traction until the spine assumes its normal shape, whereupon a metal rod can be fitted alongside the spine to prevent the scoliosis from recurring."

He clicked a switch to display the next slide. A close shot of the patient's head came into sharp focus. He was a boy of no more than ten years. Four threaded bolts connected a circular steel band to his skull. Above the boy's ears, two steel cables stretched backwards from the band. Someone sitting behind me gasped. Rita dug her nails into my palm.

"The halo, which you can see clearly in this photograph, is attached to the skull with metal bolts in a simple surgical procedure taking just a few minutes. . ."

A halo? How could he sanctify such barbarity!

Another click and a view from the back of the Stryker Bed this time. The top of the boy's head could be seen surrounded by the sinister crown, but now we could see the cables, snaking through pulleys, attached to circular weights normally associated with barbells, leather trusses, and sculptured muscles.

"Weights are added incrementally over a period of three months. . ."

A murmur rippled through the audience.

"Bolts are also attached to both sides of each knee and threaded with cables. . ."

Click. A close up of the boy's legs. Eye-bolts were screwed into either side of his knees, and taut steel wires were threaded through each of them.

Click. A view from the front of the bed this time. Weights hung from the cables attached to the boy's knees.

"Weights are attached to the leg cables so the spine is stretched from both ends."

I've never been punched in the gut by a heavyweight boxer, but right at that moment I had an inkling of how it felt. I leapt to my feet, breathing hard. "Mr Owen, have you any idea what it's like to imagine your own child attached to this barbaric apparatus? This bed looks like it belongs in the London Dungeon. Why is this necessary? Why can't you use conventional traction?" Some people clapped; others voiced their support. Mr Owen cleared his throat and sighed. I sat down.

"I fully understand the distress this might cause parents," Mr Owen began, "but it actually causes less discomfort to the patient than conventional traction, which invariably produces pressure sores. I can assure you the patient feels no pain with this procedure, and it is has proved very effective. Please, let me explain further."

He clicked to the next slide—an x-ray of a scoliotic spine. "Here you see the typical S-bend caused by scoliosis. It's compressing the liver and kidneys, and, without treatment, this patient would have died within a couple of years."

Click. Another x-ray of the same patient after surgery, viewed from the back. "After a procedure known as the Harrington rod, you see the spine is now in perfect alignment, with a metal rod inserted for additional support." The rod and surgical screws were as conspicuous as footprints in virgin snow.

Mr Owen continued with more case studies. His before-and-after photographs demonstrated far greater than words how beneficial and successful his treatment had been. His methods might be horrifying, but his results were spectacular and, above all, life-saving.

Mr Owen sat down to lukewarm applause. The photographs of the child on the Stryker Bed with the horrific steel crown would haunt my dreams. I dreaded the thought of my beloved daughter snared in such a contraption. But, if it meant saving her life. . .

"There's no way Karen's having that treatment," Rita said. Her mouth quivered.

"She may have to, love."

"No way is she having bolts screwed into her head."

"But, one day she may need this treatment to save her life."

"We'll go to another surgeon. She's not being treated by that Frankenstein." She glared at the back of Mr Owen's head.

I knew better than to argue. A lot of talking and thinking was required.

But not tonight.

-0-0-0-0-0-

By the summer of 1975, Rita and I both recognised that our growing daughter would experience increasing difficulty in managing stairs, so we decided that, finances permitting, we would need to move to a single-storey bungalow. We checked some out in the Sandfield Park area but they were well outside of our price range. Extending our radius, we found an almost new bungalow in Freshfield, a village close to the seaside town of Southport, which would suit us perfectly, except it was 25 miles from Sandfield Park! I did some digging and found that the School of the Good Shepherd, located about 5 miles from our prospective new bungalow, was similar in concept to Sandfield Park and, as luck would have it, there was a place available for Karen.

Reluctantly, we decided that, on balance, this would be a good move for the family, as the bungalow at 64 Lingdales was situated within walking distance of the National Trust's red squirrel reserve and the beach, close to shops, and close to excellent primary schools for Michael when he reached school age.

By September, we were settled into our beautiful new bungalow, which was located in a quiet cul-de-sac, and Karen had started at the Good Shepherd. Life was good… for the moment.

-0-0-0-0-0-

Karen's eyes darted like a pair of demonic bluebottles. She looked alternately at the human anatomy chart on the wall of Mr Owen's Alder Hey consulting room and the x-ray of her spine pinned to a light-box. She was clearly spooked by the difference between the ramrod-straight spine on the chart and the race track *chicane* revealed by the x-ray.

"The scoliosis appears to be progressive," Mr Owen mused. I had taken an afternoon off work to escort Karen to her first appointment with the pioneering orthopaedic surgeon. After Rita's reaction to Mr Owen's "halo" traction lecture, I had thought it wise for her to stay in Freshfield to look after Michael.

"Progressive?" I asked.

"Yes. The curve is getting worse." Mr Owen rummaged in his desk drawer, finding a pair of twelve-inch plastic rulers, before bounding over to the light-box. He placed one ruler parallel to the section of the spine above the curve and another parallel to the section below, until they intersected. "This is how we measure the angle of curvature, which you can see is about thirty degrees. Mr Strach previously measured it at twenty-five, so it appears to be progressive."

"At what point will it require surgery?" I squeezed Karen's shoulder, as she fidgeted in her wheelchair next to me.

"If the curve progresses to more than forty-five degrees, then surgery is invariably required. Of course, this kind of progression might take years… or it could deteriorate much quicker." He returned to his seat and replaced the rulers in the drawer. "Karen has a form of scoliosis associated with muscle weakness," he continued. "Because she is constantly sitting in a wheelchair, her spinal muscles have become atrophied—wasted away— causing imbalance. With scoliosis, there is a major curve and sometimes upper and lower compensating curves. In Karen's case, we have a classic double curve pattern. The major curve is convex—outside—to the right in the thoracic region…" He pointed on the anatomy chart to the part of the spine to which the ribs are attached. "and there is a compensatory left lumbar curve here." He moved his finger down the chart to the region of the lower spine. "When the curve progresses beyond forty-five degrees, the body's internal organs can become compressed and the patient's life may be endangered."

"I see." My knuckles glowed white. I clenched and unclenched my hands to relieve the pins-and-needles sensation. The thought tumbled around my brain. Karen will die if she doesn't have spinal surgery. Karen will die if… Karen will die. I shuddered. "How will you treat her."

"If the curve progresses beyond forty-five degrees, standard operating procedure is spinal fusion surgery accompanied by instrumentation to correct the deformity and provide support."

"And in the meantime?"

"No treatment is necessary at the moment," Mr Owen replied. "The curve might not progress but, I must warn you, progression is much more common in girls and, if there is significant curvature by the age of ten..." He checked his notes. "...and Karen is nine and a half now, there is likely to be a large curve at skeletal maturity. I will see Karen every six months to monitor the scoliosis and we'll see how it goes. All right, Karen?" He turned towards my daughter for the first time. "I'll see you again in six months." He smiled, but Karen didn't notice.

She was still staring at the x-ray.

-0-0-0-0-0-

Coincidently, Robert Owen was born in Chwilog, the very place where Michael was conceived, and grew up on the family farm, intending to become a vet. He was to change his mind and, after qualifying at Guy's and serving for three years in the RAF, Robert decided on a career in orthopaedics. He developed a special interest in disabilities in children and, in particular, scoliosis and he would go on to become a world-renowned professor of orthopaedics. We definitely had the right man looking after

Karen's condition.

On the way back to Freshfield, Karen was clearly preoccupied.

"What's the matter, sweetheart?" I ventured.

"I am scared, Dad. I don't want another operation."

"Don't worry, love, it's not going to happen for a long time yet."

"But my back is shaped like this…" She drew a letter S in the air with her finger.

"It will need to be corrected before it gets much worse, but Mr Owen is one of the best in the world for fixing scoliosis." Now was not the time to tell her that she may have to be fitted with the dreaded halo and strapped to a Stryker bed with weights stretching her spine. "Let's wait and see what happens."

Thirteen

My career as a computer programmer at United Biscuits started to take off and I was lucky enough to be chosen to join a fledgling process control group, which used state-of-the-art IBM System/3 computers to control processes such as the weighing of ingredients in UB factories around the country.

First, I had to learn the native assembler programming language indigenous to the System/3, which meant frequent visits to an IBM training centre in Edgbaston, Birmingham. For the first time since our marriage, I would now have to spend protracted periods at the training centre and then in factories in Harlesden (London) and Tolcross (Glasgow).

I thought I was a pretty decent programmer but something happened to disillusion me of that fanciful notion. I was in the Tolcross factory on a weekend to test my new program, which basically followed a recipe and opened valves in silos, allowing bulk ingredients such as flour and sugar to pour through into a huge weighing hopper, until the correct weight of each ingredient had been reached (taking into account the estimated weight of ingredients still falling into the hopper), when the valve would be closed. Or at least that was the theory.

I had made several dry runs with empty silos to test that the silo valves opened and closed when instructed to do so by my recipe program. Now, I was to conduct a complete system test in a "live" environment and, for obvious reasons, this had to be done when the factory was closed.

I ran the program from the System/3 console and was delighted to see flour pouring from silo 1 into the weighing hopper. This part of the process was expected to take around ten seconds and, sure enough, after holding my breath for what seemed like much longer, the silo 1 valve closed. *Yes!* Next, the valve in silo 2 opened and sugar started pouring into the ingredients hopper. Again, I held my breath and was suddenly jolted by a console message – "Catastrophic failure – process aborted." *Sugar!* With the valve waiting for a command to close that would never come, tons and tons of it continued to pour into the hopper.

I accessed my program, frantically looking for the command that would close the valve on Silo 2. I had one eye on the quickly filling hopper and was horrified to see sugar overflowing into a steadily growing heap in the middle of the factory floor. I eventually executed the command to close the valve but now there was a huge heap of sugar, about 4 feet high and spread in a wide circle. *My boss is gonna kill me!*

With no one else in attendance, I sat back in my chair and wondered how I was going to get myself out of this mess. I really didn't have a lot of options. Even if a had a wheelbarrow and shovel, I couldn't put the sugar back in the silo. I bit the bullet and telephoned my line manager, Vic Hope, who was based in London.

As I recounted the fiasco, Vic started to laugh and laugh and laugh, until I thought he would have a heart attack. When he eventually controlled himself, he said he would deal with it. He said he would call the factory manager and get a team of maintenance guys to remove the sugar.

Whew! Instead of resulting in the sack, my escapade entered company folklore, with Vic revelling in the telling of the tale.

-0-0-0-0-0-

In January of 1976, via the Link magazine, we learned of a fantastic new invention, a bicycle with a special cam, which required very little pressure on the pedals to keep it moving. A brilliant engineer, whose surname I can't remember (let's call him Mr Raleigh, after the bike manufacturer), had designed the bicycle for his son who, like Karen, was born with spina bifida. I thought this was a fantastic idea and, through the magazine, obtained the Mr Raleigh's telephone number.

Mr Raleigh (he asked me to call him Ted) was a really nice guy and invited us to his home in Nottingham to see his invention and to see his twelve-year-old son, John, riding it. We agreed to travel to Nottingham on the following Saturday and duly arrived after an uneventful 2-hour journey. In order to ride the bike, John wore specially made boots, which clipped securely onto the pedals, and the bike was equipped with stabilisers to keep it upright.

In Ted's large back garden, we eagerly awaited the demonstration. The bike looked exactly like a standard boy's two-wheeler with stabilisers, except the pedals had been replaced by stubby rods, onto which the rider's boots were clipped. There was also a circular contraption fitted around the back axle, which I learned contained the cam, the ingenious part that had to be hand-made. Ted told us that the back wheel was fixed to the pedalling mechanism, so the rider could not stop pedalling to freewheel like on a conventional bike and had no choice but to move his legs as long as the bike was moving.

Ted lifted John out of his wheelchair, sat him on the saddle, and clipped his boots onto the pedals. Then, after a gentle push from his dad to get him going, John rode around the garden and anybody watching would never know that he was paralysed from the waist down. I should explain that most of the momentum was supplied from John's hips and he rode by leaning over one side and then the other in a kind of rocking motion.

I almost begged Ted to make one for Karen and he said he would be pleased to do so at cost price, which worked out at more than £800, a lot of money in 1976. I did some quick mental arithmetic and, thanks to a recent salary increase, thought we could just about manage. Ted and I shook hands on the deal and we returned home to wait the 6 to 8 weeks it would take for the bike and the special boots to be made.

One fine Spring Saturday at the beginning of April, the bike duly arrived, together with a small pair of hand-made boots. Ted had adjusted the saddle and steering to Karen's estimated height and, when I lifted her onto the saddle, she hung onto the handlebars as if her life depended on it. I clipped her boots onto the pedals and pushed her down our path onto the road. Her legs moved as if she were pedalling the bike. As. our bungalow was situated in a circular cul-de-sac, with only one way in and out and very little traffic, I intended to push Karen slowly around the block to get her used to it.

"OK, Karen, let's start with me pushing you. We will just go once around the block and see how you get on. OK?"

"OK, Dad, but *please* don't push me too fast."

We set off at walking pace and circled Lingdales. Rita was waiting outside the house with Michael, who would be three-years-old in a few weeks.

"How was it, Karen?" Rita asked.

"It's not very comfortable, Mum, I would rather have my three-wheeler."

"Give it time, Karen," I said. "You need to get used to it. Let's go around one more time and then you can play outside on your trike."

When we returned, I unclipped Karen's boots from the pedals, lifted her onto her familiar trike, and she sped off. I sat on the bike and applied a little pressure to the pedals; they turned a few inches then whizzed round as the cam did its work. "Me 'ave go, Dad," said Michael, and I spent half an hour pushing my delighted son around Lingdales on Karen's new bike.

From this point on, I embarked on a determined crusade to teach Karen to ride her new bike and, night after night, week after week, when I returned from work, I would run for about twenty yards pushing the bike and then letting go, hoping that the momentum would be enough for Karen to start pedalling herself. She tried so hard, rocking from side to side as I had instructed but, on every occasion, the bike would inevitably slow to a standstill. I consoled myself with the knowledge that, if nothing else, her legs were being exercised as never before, so there was no way we were going to give up trying.

-0-0-0-0-0-

A couple of days before Michael's third birthday, I again accompanied Karen to Alder Hey, where she had another appointment with Mr Owen. After the obligatory visit to the Radiology department, Karen wheeled herself into Mr Owen's consulting room, where we found him studying the latest x-ray.

"The scoliosis has become more pronounced but we are not quite at the stage where surgery is required," he remarked in his appealing Welsh accent. "The bad news is that the rate of progression means surgery will almost certainly be required in a year or so. Let's see what the situation is like in another six months."

Back in Freshfield, with Karen helping Michael to complete a jigsaw on the lounge floor, Rita and I moved surreptitiously into the kitchen and I relayed the news. "We have to prepare ourselves and Karen for this surgery. Rio. It's gonna be tough on her but she will be worse off if she doesn't have it."

At Michael's third birthday party a few days later, his left eye almost closed due to an infection, we passed on the news of Karen's imminent surgery to our close family and friends, leaving out the fact that she might have to have her spine stretched beforehand. Rita and I fervently prayed that this would not be necessary but the image of the dreaded "halo" was never far from our thoughts.

Shortly afterwards, at the beginning of May, I returned home from work to find Rita in the kitchen, crying softly. "I'm not happy here, Dave, and Karen wants to go back to Sandfield Park. Can we please move back to Liverpool?" I hugged my wife and told her not to worry. We would start looking for a bungalow in South Liverpool right away.

I knew Karen loved Sandfield Park and, as she often spent 2 hours travelling to the Good Shepherd in the school bus and another 2 hours coming back, I could understand her unhappiness. The bus had to collect children from as far away as Southport and Karen was often the first to be picked up and the last to be dropped off. Of course, we were not happy about this situation but it was out of our control.

The following weekend, on Karen's 10th birthday, we visited my sister Irene and her family in Halkirk Road, Allerton, and she told me about a bungalow that had recently been put up for sale just around the corner in Melbreck Road. Rita and I almost ran there and, rather than wasting time making an appointment with the estate agent, we decided to knock and ask for a viewing. Fortunately. the owner, a Mrs. Eagle, was happy for us to look around her three-bedroomed detached property. We immediately fell in love with the bungalow and agreed to pay the asking price.

We managed to sell our Freshfield bungalow for a modest profit and towards the end of July we moved into the Melbreck Road property, which was to be our family home for the next twenty-five years. We had also arranged for Karen to return to Sandfield Park and she was due to start in September after the school's summer holiday.

In August, knowing this might be our last chance to enjoy a holiday for some considerable time, we drove to Spain's Costa Brava for our first family holiday abroad, accompanied by our close friends, Tommy and Eileen Ainscough, whose daughter, Jayne, was also born with spina bifida and who, like Karen, was a wheelchair user. They had another daughter, Carole, who was about 12-years-old at this time. Tommy towed a caravan and we had a newly-acquired tent strapped to a roof rack on our pristine Vauxhall Viva, as we wended our way south in convoy.

The trip was not without incident. As we approached Scratchwood services towards the end of the M1 motorway, Michael announced that he wanted a poo. I signalled to turn into the service area and Tommy duly followed me into the car park. I went to the boot to retrieve Michael's potty, turned the key in the lock and it snapped off flush with the lock. *Just what we needed!*

Rita took Michael to the toilet block as Tommy and I scratched our heads. It was pretty clear that we needed a new lock and I walked across to the service area, where a small workshop was attached to the petrol station. I told one of the mechanics what had happened and he agreed that a new lock was the only solution. Unfortunately, he didn't have one. He told me there was a Vauxhall dealership on the London's North Circular Road and gave me directions.

We got back on the road again and arrived at the dealership just before 5pm. Luckily, the spares shop was still open and I was able to buy a new lock. However, all of the mechanics had clocked off around 15 minutes earlier, so we would have to try to fit it ourselves. But, how were we to get the boot open?

Tommy and I got our heads together and decided that we would need to remove the back seat, remove all of our luggage and camping paraphernalia packed solidly into the boot from inside the car, activate the lock mechanism from the inside, and the boot would be open and we could fit the new lock.

A pretty good plan in theory. We managed to remove the back seat but blocking our path into the boot was a welded X-shaped divider. Using a screwdriver and hammer, I broke the weld in one corner and forced the metal strut backward, leaving a smallish gap into the boot. An hour and a half later, we had emptied our gear out of the boot and Tommy, who was more mechanically-minder than yours truly, squeezed through the gap and, flipping the closing mechanism with a screwdriver, the boot opened.

During this time, our two families had set up a picnic table on the dealership's forecourt and were eating dinner to the backdrop of heavy traffic. Not exactly what we pictured before we set off!

By 8pm, we had fitted the new lock, eaten dinner, pushed back the strut, replaced the back seat, repacked the boot, and were once more back on the road, headed for the port of Dover, where we intended to stay the night in a hotel or boarding house before catching the roll-on, roll-off ferry to Calais early the next morning.

We arrived at our destination as midnight approached and spotted a boarding house that had a "Vacancies" sign in a window. We rolled up outside and rang the bell. A dishevelled guy, clad in pyjamas, opened the door and told us the only room he had available was in the attic. Not great but we were so tired and fed up, we decided to take it. With Tommy carrying Jayne, me carrying Karen, and Rita carrying our sleeping son, and leaving the wheelchairs in the hall, we traipsed up three flights of stairs to the attic, where we found two beds between us. It was very cosy, to say the least, but we managed to grab some sleep before rising again at 7am, to the chorus of seagulls, and heading for the port and the cross-channel ferry.

Except for the torrential rain, that accompanied us through France, and

Tommy losing his wallet at our overnight camp site (we subsequently recovered it from Reception with a combination of schoolboy French and sign language), the remainder of the long drive was uneventful. We crossed the lower reaches of the Pyrenees, close to the coast, and arrived at the Spanish border where, miraculously, the sun made an appearance and accompanied us for the remainder of the holiday. We arrived at our destination in Montgo Bay, near the small town of L'Escala, in the late afternoon.

The campsite at Montgo Bay was set in a secluded orange grove, providing cooling shade for our tent and caravan, and we managed to find two adjacent pitches close to the shower and toilet block. I helped Tommy to stabilise his Super Sprite tourer caravan by winding down its four support "legs", and then it was his turn to help me put up our Cabanon frame tent. We unpacked the barbecue and soon the fragrant smell of citrus fruit was overpowered by the appetising bouquet of sizzling meat. We uncorked a bottle of Rioja and enjoyed the last of the filtered sunlight.

-0-0-0-0-0-

In November 1976, we attended Alder Hey for yet another appointment with Mr Owen and, this time, Rita and Michael accompanied Karen and me. The news was as we suspected – the scoliosis had continued its inexorable progress towards the point that would make surgery inevitable.

A nurse was commandeered to watch over Karen and Michael, while Mr Owen invited Rita and I into his consulting room. There, he advised us that two separate operations were required to straighten and fuse Karen's spinal column. The first procedure would stabilise her spine by inserting a stainless-steel rod, known as the Harrington rod, next to her spine and securing it with surgical screws, and the second would anchor Karen's pelvis to the base of her spine using what was known as Dwyer Instrumentation. The result would be a metal support for her spine shaped like an inverted "Y". He warned us that failure to carry out these procedures would lead to severe pressure on Karen's internal organs and ultimately to her premature death.

While this news was devastating, it was not unexpected. "Mr Owen, we understand that these operations are necessary to prolong Karen's life, but the most terrifying thing for us is not the two surgeries. It's the prospect of Karen having a halo screwed to her head and her spine being stretched with weights on the Stryker bed," I said. Rita's hand trembled in mine.

"I know this may sound terrifying but it's quite painless for the patient," he said. "However, in Karen's case, I don't believe it will be necessary, as I now propose to re-align her spine using orthopaedic clamps before fitting the Harrington rod. After fitting the rod, Karen will require a whole-body plaster cast for a number of months. I should also warn you that these operations will almost certainly prevent her growing to her normal height."

Despite the seriousness of the surgery, Rita and I breathed a collective sigh of relief. Our darling daughter would not need the halo fitted! I can't tell you how much comfort that brought us. Mr Owen continued, "You now have a decision to make as, if we are going to perform this surgery, it will need to be scheduled soon."

Rita and I looked at each other, both fearful. The surgery will put Karen into the hospital for a prolonged period, some of it in intensive care, and will involve a great deal of physical and psychological pain. However, failure to carry out the surgery potentially carries a much higher price, so we both made the subconscious decision to go ahead as Mr Owen had suggested.

"I don't think we have any other option but to go ahead with the surgery, Mr Owen," I eventually said. Rita nodded her head almost imperceptibly. "When will you do it?"

"We will let you know once we have made the arrangements, but I would say no later than March next year. Let Karen enjoy her Christmas first." We shook hands and left Mr Owens office to be reunited with our children. I wasn't looking forward to giving Karen the bad news. I thought that after Christmas would be as good a time as any to let her know.

"What did Mr Owen say, Dad," she asked. She was not stupid, and obviously wondered why she was not invited to join us.

"He said that your spine had bent a little more but no surgery was required just yet," I lied.

"But, you were in there a long time," she persisted.

"Yes, I know, love. He was talking about the operations that you might have to have. But you don't have to worry about that right now."

She accepted my explanation and wheeled herself out to the car with her brother hitching a lift on the back.

Fourteen

How do you explain to a ten-year-old that she has to undergo life-saving surgery? We had enjoyed a fantastic Christmas in our Melbreck Road bungalow and Karen had settled back to life at Sandfield Park School as if she had never been away. One Saturday morning in mid-January 1977, a letter arrived with the familiar NHS franking. I immediately opened it and learned that Karen's first surgery was scheduled for Tuesday 8th March and she was to be admitted on the afternoon of the preceding day. I immediately passed on this news to Rita and we agreed it was time for Karen to be told.

After breakfast, Rita and I asked Karen to come into the lounge, where Michael was obliviously playing with his Smurfs. "Karen," I began, after she had wheeled herself in. "We have just received a letter from Alder Hey telling us that you need to have an operation on your back in March." Her ubiquitous smile faded and Rita held onto her hand. "They will straighten your spine and insert a metal rod to keep it straight. After you have had the operation, you will be in a special plaster-cast and, when your back has had time to heal, you will be able to come home for a while, before going back in to have another operation." Tears streamed down her face. Rita lifted her out of her wheelchair and cuddled her on her lap.

"I'm sorry, sweetheart," I said, squeezing Karen's arm. "If you don't have these operations, your back will bend even more, you won't be able to sit up straight, and you won't be able to ride your bike."

When Karen had partly regained her composure, she whispered, "Why do I need to be in a plaster-cast, Dad?"

"It will keep your body straight while your back heals," I replied.

"How long will it be on for," she countered.

"I don't know, love. We will have to wait and see. To cheer you up, I have a surprise for you."

"What is it, Dad?"

"We are going out this afternoon to collect your new… puppy! He's a Springer Spaniel."

Karen squealed in delight.

"What shall we call him, Karen?"

She scrunched her face in deep thought and finally asked, "Can we call him Benny?"

So it was that we added Benny, an 8-week-old Springer Spaniel (or Dinger Daniel, as Michael would have it), to our family and he quickly became much loved. The Springer Spaniel was originally bred as a gun-dog, flushing out game birds by "springing" at them, and we found Benny to be a lively, intelligent, affectionate, child-friendly pooch, who loved running around and playing with his ball in our back garden. He required a lot of exercise and it became incumbent on Rita to take him out during the working week and he would accompany us on family outings on the weekends. One of our favourite locations at this time was Delamere Forest, which was littered with walking trails. Benny loved foraging in the forest, sometimes disappearing for minutes on end, and often returning with a fallen branch clamped in his jaws.

-0-0-0-0-0-

The afternoon of 7th March 1977 arrived all too quickly. Except for Benny, who had been left at my sister Irene's house, we reported "en famille" to Alder Hey's Admissions Unit at 10am as instructed and, after the paperwork was out of the way, including the signing of a consent form authorising the Harington rod surgery, we were taken to the orthopaedic ward by a chatty young porter, who pushed Karen ahead of us. His name was Alan and Karen asked him lots of personal questions, like "how old are you?", which Alan seemed happy to answer. On arrival at the ward, Karen was allocated a bed and the ward sister said that Mr Owen would be here to see us very shortly.

Mr Owen arrived and, while Karen was helping Michael to complete a jigsaw, he explained what would happen. "You already know that we are going to straighten Karen's spine and insert a Harrington rod to stabilise it. But, when Karen is in recovery, she will be covered in plaster, from shoulder to toe, to create a plaster cast in the shape of her body. When the cast has set, it is removed using a special saw, which cuts through each side, creating top and bottom sections. Each of these sections is then padded with foam to create a plaster 'bed', which sits on a special frame on top of a standard hospital bed. Karen will lie on the plaster bed for the next 8 to 10 weeks, until everything has settled down."

"That's a long time to be lying on a bed," I interrupted and Karen's eyes widened.

"Yes, it certainly is and there is a risk of pressure sores forming so, to stop this happening, every two hours, the porters will turn the bed over. So, let's say Karen is lying on her back on the bottom section, the top piece will be placed on her body and secured with straps, before being rotated so she will now be lying on her front. The straps are then removed and the section she was originally lying on is taken off. Two hours later, the procedure is repeated in reverse, so she will be alternately lying on her back then her front."

"You mentioned previously that Karen would be in the Intensive Care Unit immediately after the operation," Rita said. "How long will she be there for?"

"Yes, we are talking about major surgery lasting for several hours. So, Karen will be in the ICU for two or three days and closely monitored, before returning to the orthopaedic ward," Mr Owen finished. "Any more questions?"

Rita and I looked at each other. "I don't think so, Mr Owen, thank you," I said eventually.

He bid us goodbye and told Karen he would see her in the morning. Karen, of course, had overheard this conversation and, as soon as Mr Owen left, she began to cry, softly at first, progressing to huge shuddering sobs. I lifted Michael off the bed and Rita replaced him, cuddling Karen until her sobs subsided.

Before too long, Karen was back in her wheelchair and chatting to the nursing staff with whom she formed an immediate rapport, boding well for what was going to be a long stay. We were allowed to stay with Karen until the evening visiting session finished at 8pm and we eventually tip-toed out while she was telling one of the nurses about the bicycle she was trying to learn to ride. As we left, the ward sister told us we could return at 8am to be with Karen before she was taken to the operating theatre.

-0-0-0-0-0-

When we arrived a little before 8am the next day, Karen was awake but drowsy from the recently-administered pre-operative sedative, and she appeared to have resigned herself to the operation with her usual brave face. At 8:30, two porters, one of whom was Alan, wheeled a trolley to Karen's bed and she was quickly transferred and wheeled out towards the nearby operating theatres. We stayed with her as far as the double-doors leading to the theatre suite, kissed and hugged her, telling her not to worry, that everything was going to be alright. When Karen disappeared inside, Rita could not prevent the rivers of tears that streamed down her face and I quickly walked Michael away. "Shall we go for a drink in the café while we are waiting for Karen to come back?" I asked him. "Yes please, Dad! Can I have juice?"

The next 8 hours were the longest we had ever experienced. We sat in the café, walked in the grounds, crossed over to the nearby Eaton Road shops, then back to the café and began the cycle again. For the first few hours, Michael was quite happy playing with his toys, colouring in pictures, or assembling his wooden jigsaw puzzle, but he started to become bored. "When will Karen be back, Dad?" he asked. "I don't know, son, but it shouldn't be too long now," was the best I could say. Ever so slowly, the 4pm visiting period came around and we returned to the orthopaedic ward, where we were allowed to wait and, around an hour later, one of the nurses told us that Karen was out of theatre, that the surgery had gone well, and that she was currently awake in the recovery room. Within the next hour she would be transferred to the Intensive Care Unit.

As the time reached 6:30pm and we had heard no more, we decided to go to the ICU to enquire if Karen had arrived. A nurse intercepted us before we could reach the unit proper and abruptly asked what we were doing there. "We are Karen Verinder's family," I replied. "She should be here by now after her surgery."

She hurried off to check and soon returned. "Karen has only just got here and we are still setting up her monitoring equipment. You will be able to see her in about fifteen minutes." I thanked the nurse and she showed us to the Parents' Lounge. Michael sat on the floor and wheeled his toy car in circles.

When we were finally summoned into the inner sanctum, we found Karen sleeping soundly on her back on the promised plaster bed, with tubes snaking out of both arms, another from her back, draining blood from the surgical site into a bottle, and with a bunch of wires connecting her to a heart monitor. She was breathing through an oxygen mask and, except for looking a little pale, she seemed to have coped with the surgery pretty well. The ICU was surprisingly noisy, with bleeps and whooshes providing a constant clamour. After 30 minutes of watching Karen softly snoring, we decided to leave her to sleep off the anaesthetic.

-0-0-0-0-0-

At around 7am the following morning, I rang the ICU and the ward sister told me that Karen was wide awake and chatting as if nothing had happened. She was in no pain and the porters would be there at 8 o'clock to turn Karen's plaster bed for the first time, returning every two hours throughout the day and night. I let Rita know the good news and arranged to pick her up at around 3:30pm, allowing plenty of time to get to the ICU for afternoon visiting. Rita planned to leave Michael with her Mum, as the

ICU was not a great place for an almost-four-year-old to spend time.

I set off for work earlier than usual, so that I could get as much done as possible before having to leave at 3 o'clock and I had arranged with my London-based boss to work out of the Liverpool office for the next 2 or 3 months. My colleagues and friends at United Biscuits were among the best people I have ever worked with. The IT department, in particular, was a tight-knit group of highly-motivated, young professionals and I loved working there.

When we arrived at the ICU, two new porters were in the process of turning Karen and we paused to watch them do their work. They were laughing and joking with her throughout the process and she later told us she actually looked forward to the two-hourly porters' visits, especially when Alan was on duty. Porters are probably rated pretty low in Alder Hey's hierarchy but, in our experience, they do a fantastic job, especially in cheering the children up.

Turning the plaster bed sounded straight-forward in theory, but Karen was connected to drips and monitors and she also had a drain inserted into the operation site, so it was a little tricky, requiring the help of a nurse to disconnect what could be disconnected and connecting them back again. Presently, the porters finished turning the plaster bed and left the ICU.

We approached Karen's bed, but she couldn't see us until we were at her bedside because she was now lying on her front. "Hi sweetheart, how are you feeling," I asked. Her cheeks were a rosy pink and, considering she had recently endured a major surgical procedure, she looked very well.

"I am OK, Dad. My back is a bit sore, but it's not too bad." Rita and I leaned forward in turn and kissed her cheek. "Well, you look great," Rita laughed, "Are you sure you have had an operation?" Rita, too, looked much better than she had for days. There had been little point in telling her not to worry as that is what parents do, especially mums, but Rita now looked as though a huge weight had been lifted from her shoulders. Me, too, I guess.

We chatted for a while and I left Rita at Karen's bedside while I looked for the ward sister, the unit's head nurse. The nursing staff in the ICU were incredibly busy, with one nurse dedicated to each patient, and other nurses providing backup services. I found the dark-blue-uniformed sister instructing a trainee nurse in the management of a saline drip. "Sister, do you have a minute, please," I ventured. "Yes, I'll be with you shortly," she replied. Eventually she turned to me and asked, "What can I do for you?"

"I am Karen's dad", I replied.

"Oh, hello Mr Verinder. Karen is doing remarkably well. The operation went according to plan and we will probably transfer her to the orthopaedic ward sometime tomorrow."

"That's great news", I said. "We were expecting her to be in the ICU until Friday at the earliest."

"Karen has made a great recovery from the anaesthetic and the physical trauma of her operation. We will be sad to see her go as she has been a delightful patient, never complaining, and always so cheerful and chatty."

"Thanks, sister, I will let you get back to your work."

I wended my way back to Karen's bedside and said, "Great news, Karen. Tomorrow they will disconnect all of the tubes and you will be transferred back to the orthopaedic ward. The sister said you have been a model patient." Rita squeezed Karen's hand and they exchanged happy mother-daughter smiles.

As promised, on the Thursday after her operation, Karen was wheeled into the orthopaedic ward aboard her plaster bed, and so began many weeks of routine on Karen's journey of recovery. In the orthopaedic ward, parents and siblings could visit at any time and other family and friends could visit between 2pm and 7pm, so Karen was never short of visitors. United Biscuits' Liverpool office was just short 10-minute drive from Alder Hey, so it was relatively easy for me to pop in to see Karen two or three times a day. As for Rita, she spent most of her day with Karen, sometimes with Michael for company, but mostly Michael was left with Rita's Mum and she would collect him at around 6pm, after I had relieved her at the hospital.

A couple of weeks into her hospitalisation, Karen continued her education with daily weekday visits from a mobile female schoolteacher, although I am not sure how much work actually got done, as Karen could chat for England, losing no opportunity to change the subject from Maths and English to social chit-chat.

This wasn't a great time for Benny, the Springer Spaniel, who was often left alone for long periods. Fortunately, he was now toilet-trained and didn't foul up the house, while we were gone. I would routinely head home at around 1pm to take Benny for a walk and let him take care of business and, before collecting Michael in the early evening, Rita would again take Benny out to relieve himself.

The two-hourly turning of the plaster bed, day and night, would become routine for Karen and, if I am honest, I don't think I could have endured it quite so well, especially during the night. Being woken up every two hours during the night, week after week, would make a saint grumpy, but Karen never complained and Rita and I were so proud of her.

After around four weeks in the orthopaedic ward, weekend weather permitting, the porters would lift Karen's plaster bed onto a hospital trolley and we would wheel her into the hospital grounds and have a family picnic on one of the beautifully-manicured lawns.

Towards the end of April 1977, a few days after Michael's 4th birthday and almost seven weeks after her operation, Karen was discharged from hospital, returning home by ambulance on a trolley with the plaster bed aboard. Rita and I would have to turn Karen every four hours, night and day but, at last, the arduous trips to Alder Hey, and the disruption to our everyday lives this caused, were no longer required.

-0-0-0-0-0-

Benny habitually shared Karen's plaster bed, often sleeping across her legs, and he was not best pleased when we interrupted his sleep to turn Karen in the middle of the night. Rita was now Karen's nurse as well as her Mum and she invested a lot of time massaging her with talcum powder after each turn of the plaster bed to help ward off the omnipresent danger of pressure sores. Rita had no formal training but she intuitively knew what Karen needed and she was a quite brilliant nurse. Each morning, with Karen lying on her back, Rita would wash her down and dress her in her usual clothes, which was not easy with Karen unable to be moved from her prone position. Also, for Karen, eating while lying flat on her back was particularly difficult and she must have been sick of the soft food she was slowly spoon-fed. She could actually feed herself when lying on her front and, in this position, she could also drink through a straw without choking.

With Karen back at home, life returned to something resembling normal, and she enjoyed spending time in the garden watching her brother play with Benny, laughing at their antics. I would help turn Karen before setting off for work, returning at lunchtime and early evening to do the same. We soon established a routine and, thanks mainly to Rita's ministrations, Karen did not develop any pressure sores, commonly known as bed sores, which are notoriously difficult to heal. Pressure sores are basically injuries to the skin caused by prolonged pressure to the same area and are most often experienced by people confined to bed for long periods.

For Karen's 11th birthday on 8th May, we planned a small house party for close family and friends and, even though she was confined to her plaster bed, she enjoyed a great laughter-filled day. More than anything else, she loved being with her family and friends and she especially loved family parties, when everyone she loved were together in the same place.

Although we savoured the warm summer months, Karen's imminent return to Alder Hey for a second major operation was never far from our minds. We ventured outside a few times when the sun was shining but we couldn't go far because pushing the trolley along the pavement, with the plaster bed aboard, was slow, back-breaking work. With Rita looking after Michael and walking Benny on a lead, I was Karen's "pusher" and I was terrified of jolting her back.

The Merseyside Police Dog & Mounted Section was located about half-a-mile from our Melbreck Road bungalow and, each summer, they held a public demonstration day, where the dogs and horses would show off their skills. This year, it was held on a sunny Saturday in July and we managed to manoeuvre Karen's trolley into the showground without mishap. In fact, Karen was the centre of attention, meeting many friends and neighbours who hadn't seen her for some time. She even had her photograph taken with the star police dog, a huge German shepherd, kindly arranged by one of our friends, Ken Wagner, who was himself a dog handler with Merseyside Police.

After her discharge from hospital at the end of April, Karen had to make out-patient visits to Alder Hey every 6 weeks, transported on her trolley via ambulance. Mr Owen was delighted with her progress and, on the second visit, he told us that, as far as he was concerned, Karen was now ready to have the second operation, the so-called Dwyer Instrumentation, named after the Australian surgeon, Allen Dwyer, which would anchor the base of Karen's spine firmly to her pelvis. He would start the ball rolling and we would be informed of the date of the operation by letter.

The letter arrived a week later and the operation was scheduled for Tuesday 8th August, with Karen needing to be admitted on the preceding Monday afternoon. We arrived at the Admissions Unit at 2pm and signed the consent form, before a couple of young porters pushed Karen's trolley to the orthopaedic ward and transferred her and the plaster bed onto her designated hospital bed. Mr Owen arrived about an hour later.

"How are you, Karen?" he asked.

"I'm s…s…scared," she stuttered.

"Don't worry," Mr Owen said. "We will take good care of you. Mum and Dad, do you have any questions about the surgery?"

"Will Karen still have to be on the plaster bed after this op?" Rita asked.

"No, her spine is now securely fused and the rod will keep it straight. After the Dwyer Instrumentation, all she will need is a surgical corset, which will provide extra support for her back while the procedure settles down."

"Will she have to go to the ICU afterwards?" I asked.

"Yes, just as a precaution. This is another major operation and we will monitor her closely for the first 24 hours. All being well, she will then be transferred back to the orthopaedic ward, where we will monitor her progress over the coming weeks. If everything goes according to plan, after four to six weeks, Karen should be able to continue her recovery at home. She will need to wear the surgical corset for the next twelve months or so but, after that, she will not need it, as her spine should be firmly supported."

"Thank you so much, Mr Owen," I said. His skill had given Karen a new lease on life and we were so grateful to him and his team.

The remainder of the afternoon passed uneventfully. We had left Michael and Benny with Rita's Mum and we were able to devote our time to Karen, playing Hangman and any other game that would take her mind off the upcoming operation. When we eventually left her, she was chatting to the teenage girl in the next bed and didn't appear to notice we had gone.

The next morning, we followed a similar procedure to her previous surgery, leaving a lightly-sedated Karen to Mr Owen's expert care outside the doors to the operating theatre suite, where a theatre nurse held her hand as she was wheeled in. This time, though, we didn't wait around for the six or seven hours the surgery was scheduled to take. I dropped Rita off at her Mum and Dad's house, arranging to pick her up again at 3pm, and I drove to United Biscuits to take care of some urgent amendments to a program that weighed packets of biscuits coming off the production line and dumped underweight packets into a bin by activating a hydraulic ram. After the ignominy of the Tolcross fiasco, I was particularly careful to ensure my code was subjected to a rigorous testing regime.

I picked Rita up on schedule and arrived at the ICU Parents' Lounge at about 3:30pm. The receptionist told us that Karen was in Recovery and was expected to be transferred to the ICU within the next hour. I suppose we had become inured to the stress because, this time, we were not nearly so nervous as the previous time. We knew what to expect and were not surprised when Karen was wheeled into the ICU connected to tubes and monitors. Like the previous time, she was sleeping and breathing through an oxygen mask. A blood transfusion was dripping slowly into one arm and a saline solution was trickling into the other. A drain snaked from her lower back to a bottle partly filled with blood. It took me a little while to notice that Karen was not lying on her plaster bed. Instead, her body was wrapped in the promised surgical corset.

We sat with Karen for an hour but she continued to sleep soundly. We left after being reassured by the sister in charge of the ICU that the operation had gone according to plan and Karen was recovering well. She also told us that, if Karen continued her rate of recovery, she was likely to be transferred to the orthopaedic ward tomorrow evening or shortly after.

-0-0-0-0-0-

I rang the ICU at around 7am the next morning and was relieved to hear that Karen had slept through most of the night and was now propped up in bed, enjoying a light breakfast, and she was expected to be disconnected from her drips and heart monitor and transferred to the orthopaedic ward that afternoon. We dropped Michael and Benny off at Rita's Mum's house again and drove to Alder Hey through the rush-hour traffic, arriving at the ICU at about 8:15am.

Karen was a little pale and her back ached but Rita and I were amazed at how well she looked after such traumatic surgery. I stayed for an hour before leaving for work but Rita stayed with Karen and was still there when I returned at about 1:30pm. Karen now had more colour in her cheeks and had even managed to eat some scrambled eggs.

"How does it feel to be off the plaster bed, Karen?" I asked.

"it's great, Dad. I can sit up a bit now and see what's going on." She continued, "The nurse said I should be able to go back to the orthopaedic ward later."

"That's good news. You'll be back in your wheelchair in no time."

An hour later, I had to go back to work but Rita wanted to stay. "We'll see you at the 6 o'clock visiting time in the ward," she said, as I kissed them both goodbye.

When we met up again, it was in the orthopaedic ward and, as I strolled past the ward sister's office, she called me in for a quick chat.

"Mr Owen usually does his ward rounds between 10 and 11am and, if you want to, you can be here to hear what he has to say and you can ask him any questions you may have related to Karen's surgery," she offered.

"That's fine sister," I replied, "my wife and I will be here. Thanks a lot."

At Karen's bedside, I noticed the only remaining tube was the drain from her back. I relayed the sister's message, then Rita and I helped Karen with her puzzle book until it was time to leave.

-0-0-0-0-0-

We arrived back at 10 o'clock the next morning and were pleased to see Mr Owen enter the ward with his entourage at a little after 10:15. Mr Owen, together with his registrar and a gaggle of student doctors soon surrounded Karen's bed. The surgeon briefly checked Karen's chart and turned to us.

"The operation went very well and Karen is recovering nicely," he commented. "I am just about to look at the x-ray taken immediately after the surgery. Would you like to join me?"

"That would be great, Mr Owen," I replied.

We followed him and his team to a lightbox on the wall close to the sister's office. Mr Owen pulled the x-ray out of its manilla folder, clipped it to the box, and turned on the light.

I stared at the x-ray and Rita squeezed my hand tightly. The spine with its fused vertebrae was clearly visible and was now ramrod straight. A metal rod was clipped to the top and bottom vertebrae and surgical screws or bolts also attached the rod to the spine in a number of places in between. This was the Harrington rod. My gaze shifted to the lower back area, where two smaller rods and wires bridged the gap between spine and pelvis. The Dwyer Instrumentation. The overall effect was that of an upturned letter "Y". It was quite simply an astonishing piece of surgical engineering.

As Rita and I continued to stare at the image, Mr Owen explained to the student doctors how he had performed the procedures, using lots of jargon I didn't understand, and pointing to various parts of the instrumentation as he spoke. The students seemed enthralled and were taking copious notes as he wound up his talk.

He turned to Rita and I. "As you can see, the spine is now straight and well supported both vertically with the rod and horizontally with the Dwyer instrumentation. I expect Karen to make a complete recovery and don't expect any recurrence of the scoliosis."

"It's fantastic, Mr Owen. We can't thank you enough," I said. He simply nodded and led us back to Karen's bed.

"Well, Karen," he said, "The operation went according to plan and you are recovering as expected. We will monitor your progress and, all being well, you should be able to go home in about 4 weeks."

He wished us a good day and moved on to his next patient.

"Mr Owen has done a great job with your back, Karen!" I beamed. "Your spine is now straight and he said there was very little chance of the scoliosis happening again."

"When will I be able to go back in my wheelchair, Dad?" she asked.

"Mr Owen didn't say, love, but why don't you ask him when he next comes to see you? He should be back tomorrow morning and you can ask him then."

When Mr Owen had left the ward, the sister approached Karen's bed. "Well, Mum and Dad, what do you think of Mr Owen's handiwork?"

"It's fantastic, Sister," I said, with an adrenalin rush. "It's hard to believe, considering how much Karen's spine had curved. It's like he's installed a sort of internal scaffolding! We can't thank him enough."

"Yes, he's a brilliant surgeon," she replied. "He can be a bit abrupt sometimes but he is performing miracles for his patients." She paused and her smile faded. "I hate to spoil your mood but you will have to go now before Matron does her rounds. We'll see you again at visiting time, if that's OK?"

"No problem, Sister," I said. "Thanks again for allowing us to see Mr Owen."

She left us to say goodbye to Karen, and Rita and I left the ward buoyed by the success of Karen's surgeries.

As previously, the days following the latest operation became routine. A week after her Dwyer surgery, Karen was allowed to spend time in her wheelchair and, interspaced with regular tuition from the mobile teaching staff, she habitually spent her days roaming around the ward, making new friends, chatting with the porters (wearing a huge smile whenever Alan made an appearance!), and gossiping with the nurses on their breaks. Five weeks later, Mr Owen decreed that she could continue her recovery at home, providing she attended regular out-patient appointments so he could keep a watchful eye on her progress.

Fifteen

Karen was, of course, delighted to be home again. In her spare time, she could now listen to her favourite Elvis records and watch her ever-expanding collection of Elvis movies, starting with his Love Me Tender debut through to his last role as Dr John Carpenter in Change of Habit, and many of them in between. From an early age, since Rita and I first introduced her to Elvis, she became obsessed with him and she was absolutely devastated when her hero died on the 16th August 1977, just eight days after her Dwyer surgery. She was among the legion of fans who mourned Elvis's passing and one of her great ambitions in life was to visit the great man's Graceland home in Memphis, Tennessee, where he was subsequently buried. Many years later, she was able to satisfy this ambition.

Karen continued to wear her surgical corset under her regular clothes, resuming her studies at Sandfield Park, and we settled down to a regular family routine for the first time in many months. However, one Saturday afternoon in the first week of October, our peace was shattered. Our Melbreck Road bungalow backed on to the Liverpool to London inter-city railway line and an inquisitive Benny, playing alone in the garden, managed to scale the high boundary wall. When we belatedly realised he was missing, I found him fifty yards up the track, lying on his side, not moving. He had obviously been hit by a train and, when I reached him, one of his back legs was bent at an unnatural angle. As I began to lift his body from the side of the track, I heard a low whimpering sound and realised he was still alive.

I drove him to the local vet and, after a thorough examination, his only serious injury was a broken back leg, which was set, splinted, and bound, and Benny was good to go. He was in quite a lot of pain and felt very sorry for himself. The vet gave him a pain-killing injection and gave me some tablets to give to him later when the effects of the injection had worn off.

Back home, I placed Benny on his side in his basket and he promptly curled up and was soon fast asleep. Six weeks later and Benny was as good as new. However, a month or so after he had regained full fitness, while out for an evening walk, our bad luck with pets continued, as Benny, whom Rita had trained to walk at heel, was run over by a car while chasing a cat across the road. This time poor Benny could not be saved.

However, our luck soon changed for the better. The summer after Benny's demise, I returned home one evening after a football training session to find a young golden Labrador lying on our front lawn. As I moved closer, I could see that the poor dog was emaciated and, when I tried to stroke her head, she cringed away from me. She was severely malnourished and, judging by her fear, she had been badly treated by her former owner. She was not wearing a collar and appeared to have been dumped on the street to fend for herself.

I tried to comfort her and, eventually, she trusted me enough to follow me to our back door. I shouted Rita and she quickly appeared, arching her eyebrows as she spotted the dog.

"I found her on the front lawn. The poor dog is starving and she is on heat." I said. "Do we have anything for her to eat?"

"I can warm up some beef soup," Rita replied.

Rita placed the bowl of soup just outside the back door and the dog wolfed it down. I then filled another bowl with water and set that down next to the soup bowl. She lapped it up in a few seconds. It was almost dark now, but the evening was balmy, so we decided to leave her outside with the gate open so that she could move on if she wanted to.

Early the next morning, I opened the back door to find the dog sound asleep on the step. She had found a new home. Karen and Michael were delighted and we decided to call the dog Sandy. She desperately needed a bath, which we eventually managed despite her skittishness She cringed at any sudden hand movement and it took quite a while to get her to trust us. Rita bought some dog food from the local convenience store and soon Sandy was fed and watered. During a visit to the vet, she was vaccinated against canine diseases and, thankfully, she was not pregnant. The vet guessed her age to be between nine and twelve months and, as she was to be a family pet, he recommended that she be spayed as soon as her "heat" had finished.

Sandy soon reached her normal weight, her golden coat glistening with good health, and she became a much-loved member of the family.

-o-0-0-0-0-

So began a long period of stability as far as Karen's health was concerned. She didn't let her disability affect her ambitions. She was determined to one day get a job, learn to drive, and have her own home, all of which, in the fullness of time, she would achieve.

Unfortunately, Karen was unable to ride her bike by herself. No matter how many times we tried, after giving her a push start, she ground to an inexorable halt. Realising we were flogging a dead donkey, we eventually stopped trying and gave the bike to another spina bifida sufferer, who was able to master the rolling technique required to keep the bike moving.

In September 1978, at the age of five, Michael began his education at Booker Avenue Junior School. One thing I should mention about our much-loved son was the fact that he never once asked why Karen was in a wheelchair. He simply accepted her as she was. Rita and I were determined that Karen would not be defined by her disability and, it seemed, we had unconsciously passed this on to Michael. He always referred to Karen as his sister and never as his disabled sister. We were often surprised by the reaction of Michael's friends when meeting Karen for the first time, as it was clear they weren't aware that Karen was a wheelchair user.

The following summer, a friend of Rita's told her that there was a job available at Booker Avenue school, assisting a number of disabled children. Rita immediately applied for and got the job, starting in September 1979, and her first charges were a precocious seven-year-old Debbie Jones, who was also born with spina bifida, another young female spina bifida sufferer called Laura Monk, and two boys named Jamie Kavanagh and Barry Hughes. Rita's job was to look after the welfare of her "kids" during the school day. She had no formal qualifications but she had thirteen years of practical experience that made her the ideal candidate.

Debbie, who could get around on crutches and used her wheelchair only as a backup, was more mobile than Karen, but she still needed help from Rita from time to time, especially when visiting the toilet block, which had no special provisions for the disabled. Over a period of years, Debbie and her lovely family became our life-long friends, with Debbie and Karen forging a particularly strong bond that was to last until Debbie's premature death at the age of 44.

Laura was also more mobile than Karen, using elbow crutches to help her move around the school, and Jamie, a talented trumpet player who eventually formed his own brass band, had quite severe scoliosis. Barry suffered from cerebral palsy and his walking and speech were adversely affected. So, as well as looking after her own daughter, Rita now had four other young people with a range of disabilities and special needs to look after. She thoroughly enjoyed her work and was soon a familiar figure to all of the children at Booker Avenue.

-0-0-0-0-0-

At this time, in the late 1970s, there were very few facilities for wheelchair users. The places that were easily accessible to the general public, such as libraries and cinemas, were difficult or impossible to access if you were a wheelchair user. There were very few ramps and disabled toilets, so we had to improvise. On one occasion, in September '78, Karen and I went to the Allerton Odeon cinema to see Grease, starring John Travolta and Olivia Newton-John. The ticket office was at the top of a flight of ten steps so I did what I always did in these situations. I turned the wheelchair around and dragged it backwards one step at a time to the top. Over the years, I had done this hundreds of times and, if I may say so, I was pretty good at it. At the ticket office, I bought one adult and one child ticket and headed towards the auditorium, the entrance to which was up another steep flight of stairs. As I began to turn the wheelchair to climb the stairs, the cinema manager approached at a lick. "I am sorry, sir, but you can't take a wheelchair into the cinema as it is against the fire regulations." he whined.

"We have been here many times before," I reasoned. "In fact, this will be the third time we have been to see this film in this cinema during the past two weeks."

"Well you can't come in today or any time in the future." he replied.

I thought for a second. "OK," I said, "Here's what we are going to do. You are going to get out of my way and I will take my daughter up these stairs. And, if the cinema should spontaneously combust while the film is in progress, I will wheel my daughter out of the fire exit close to the screen where there are no steps at all, OK?"

I spun the wheelchair without waiting for an answer, catching his leg with a footrest, and he hopped out of the way. I dragged the wheelchair to the top of the stairs and he stayed at the bottom rubbing his shin.

This is just one example of the barriers that were in our way at this time and, rightly or wrongly, my attitude on hitting one of these hurdles was to find a way to jump over it or move around it. I didn't see why Karen should be denied the simple pleasure of watching a film at her local cinema. I understand that there have to be rules and regulations but common sense should prevail. Believe me, if there had been a fire in the cinema during the showing of Grease, Karen and I would have been among the first to get out!

When we were at home in our bungalow, Karen could transfer from her wheelchair to the toilet and back again using her considerable upper-body strength to "jump" across the gap. However, when we were out, let's say at a restaurant, if Karen needed the toilet, quite often the wheelchair would not fit through the door or the toilet would not be big enough to accommodate the wheelchair. In these situations, either Rita or I would lift Karen from her wheelchair onto the toilet and Rita would stay with her while she took care of business. I would remain outside with the wheelchair until Karen was ready to be lifted back on. We accepted this as the norm and it would be many years before things changed for the better.

On a melancholy note, towards the end of 1978, we heard that Alan, the young Alder Hey porter, had been tragically killed in a motorcycle accident. He was a sad loss to the unofficial Guild of Hospital Porters. He had helped make Karen's long stays in Alder Hey more bearable and she was inconsolable at this news.

-0-0-0-0-0-

During her teenage years, Karen showed no signs of the so-called "terrible teens". She craved independence, wanting to experience everything that her able-bodied equivalents could experience, and Rita and I were determined to help her achieve this goal.

The staff at Sandfield Park seemed to share our views, as extracurricular activities included events such as horse riding and abseiling. Karen loved these outings and was not fazed in the least at the thought of lowering herself down a vertical cliff face!

Sandfield Park and Karen were a great match and she loved the teaching and caring staff, especially a young teacher named Sue O'Neill, with whom she enjoyed a special relationship. Because Karen had missed so much schooling due to long stays in hospital, she was allowed to stay on at the school for an extra year and she finally left, aged seventeen, with 3 GCSEs and many years of happy memories. Karen was not particularly academic but her physical well-being and happiness were more important to us. Rita and I will always be grateful to everyone at Sandfield Park for the sterling help and support they provided during Karen's sojourn there.

Some years after Karen's birth, I learned that many spina bifida sufferers had some form of learning difficulty, especially in subjects such as mathematics and reading, but Karen had no such difficulties. In fact, by the time she was three-years-old, she could read better than many older children. She learned using some rudimentary "flash" cards I made out of scrap cardboard and constant practice meant she could read a newspaper by the time she started school.

Sixteen

After leaving Sandfield Park, Karen joined the Greenbank Project, a government-funded initiative to help young disadvantaged and disabled adults to integrate, gain vocational qualifications, and work experience, which they hoped would lead to full-time employment. At this time, the Project was headed by Gerry Kinsella, himself a wheelchair user, who understood the difficulties and prejudices that disabled people faced, and he and his staff worked tirelessly to provide opportunities for their young charges. Rita and I thought it was a great project and were delighted when Karen was offered a place. The aim of the project was to create both a higher-education College and a Sports Academy, offering such diverse courses as Catering, Art & Design, Textiles, Business & Administration, Information Technology, Hairdressing, Health & Fitness, Gardening, and Sports Coaching & Development. Karen chose the Business & Administration course, where she would learn skills such as touch-typing, filing, making and receiving telephone calls, and using office equipment including computers, photocopiers, and fax machines.

While studying at Greenbank, Karen celebrated her eighteenth birthday with a party at the beautiful Reynolds Park venue in Woolton. As she revelled in the company of her family and friends, I recalled the trauma of her birth, when she was not expected to live for 24 hours, and here we were, 18 years later, and she was glowing with vitality, the picture of good health. Except for her disability, she was a typical eighteen-year-old, who meticulously (and expertly) applied make up, dressed to impress, and was interested in music, fashion, football, and boys and not necessarily in that order!

Our precious daughter had reached adulthood. Rita and I had done all we could to make her life a happy one and I doubt anyone could have done more. In particular, Rita had been the most devoted mother that Karen could have had. Although we would always be there for her, from now on she would make her own decisions, her own mistakes, and live her own life the way she wanted to live it.

So far, I have neglected to mention Karen's love of Liverpool Football Club. I am from a long line of fervent Liverpool supporters and, of course, I passed this passion on to Karen and Michael. When Karen was in her late teens, in the mid-1980s, she got to meet one of her heroes, Craig Johnston, Liverpool's curly-haired Australian winger, affectionately known as "Skippy". By this time, along with my cousin, Brian Verinder, I had founded Microtech Computer Services and had organised the Microtech Half Marathon, with all proceeds going to the Greenbank Project. I also arranged for Craig Johnston to present the prizes and medals and, after the prize-giving, Craig and Karen chatted like old friends.

A keen amateur photographer, Craig offered to take a photograph of him and Karen next to his sports car, which had the registration ROO 1. Craig asked for Karen's address and said he would drop off a copy of the photograph once he had developed it. A few weeks later, returning from a Sunday afternoon outing to Delamere Forest, we found a large package on the doorstep. It was covered in brown paper and tied with string. I passed it to Karen and she tore the wrapping off, revealing the promised photograph, blown-up and tastefully framed.

"Craig has been here!" she cried. She was delighted that Craig had kept his promise but devastated that she had missed him. However, at the next Liverpool home game, Karen was with Rita in the disabled section at the front of the Paddock and, at this time, the players would routinely kick balls into the crowd before kick-off. Karen was overjoyed when Craig ran over and passed a ball to her. One of the stewards captured the moment on film for posterity. Karen thanked Craig for the photograph and was thrilled when he invited her and Rita into the Player's Lounge after the game. We will be eternally grateful to Craig Johnston for the kindness he showed to Karen.

While she was at Greenbank, Karen met a young able-bodied student called Mark and they started going out together. Mark was a good-looking boy who, I guessed, was not short of female admirers. Karen was also a very attractive young lady but, as you know, she was confined to a wheelchair and suffered the many disadvantages that came with it. This being the case, Rita and I were suspicious of Mark's motives from the beginning. However, our only concern was Karen's happiness and we couldn't choose who she was going to fall in love with.

They were together for a few months when disturbing stories started to get back to us. Karen and Mark had visited my brother Geoff's house, where Mark had apparently lifted Karen out of her wheelchair and tossed her roughly onto a settee when, given her spinal problems, she needed to be treated gently. When Geoff told me about this, I went ballistic! I wanted to kill the bastard!

So, next time he called to pick Karen up, I asked him if I could have a private word. By this time, I had calmed down but my anger was still simmering. "Mark," I began. "You know that Karen has had two major surgeries on her spine, don't you?" He nodded apprehensively, wondering where this was going. My eyes narrowed. "Well, this means that she has to be handled with extreme care, especially when she is transferring to and from her wheelchair." He shifted uncomfortably, and wouldn't meet my eyes. "I understand that you were less than gentle with Karen when you visited Geoff's house." He started to stammer something but I stopped him. "Don't say anything, just listen." I ordered. "I will put this episode down to ignorance on your part but, if you ever mistreat Karen again, then you are going to have me to deal with and I am not disabled." I glared at him as he stared at the ground. "Do you understand?"

He nodded again, still not looking at me. I didn't tell Karen about this "discussion" but, from this time forward, Rita and I would keep a much closer eye on Mark.

Another few months went by and Mark appeared to be unaware that Rita and I had made a lot of friends at the Greenbank Project since the Half Marathon and, while I was in London on business, word came back to Rita that Mark had been boasting and making what I shall simply refer to as inappropriate remarks to a group of his mates, which were overheard by one of our friends.

Mark had his own flat at this time and Rita was not going to let this lie. Without Karen's knowledge, she went to see him. The following is what Rita told me took place. She grabbed him around the throat, while simultaneously kneeing him in the groin, and as he moaned in agony, she whispered in his ear. "Guess why I am here? I know what you have been saying to your mates and, when I have gone, you are going to phone Karen and tell her that you are finished." She tightened her grip around his throat while he was still clutching his balls. "If you ever contact Karen again, you will wish you had never been born." She reluctantly let go of his throat and stormed off.

We never saw Mark again and he was not seen again at the Greenbank Project either. The downside was that Karen was absolutely heartbroken and we really felt for her. Of course, we couldn't tell her what had happened, otherwise she would have been even more upset. We comforted her the best we could but it took a very long time for her to get over her heartbreak. From this time forward, she would always compare her disabled suitors with "Saint" Mark and, in her eyes, there was no comparison. In the meantime, she would continue to wait for the next Mark to come into her life.

-0-0-0-0-0-

When Karen was eighteen, she began to learn to drive at a specialist driving school for disabled drivers. A year later, her instructor thought she was ready to take her driving test and she duly applied. Unfortunately, she failed but she was nothing if not determined. She took her driving test three more times with the same result but at the 5th attempt she finally passed!

She had reached another milestone on her path to independence. We rewarded her triumph by buying her a car, a Nissan Micra with hand controls and a streamlined rooftop box, which housed an automated mechanism designed to lift her folded wheelchair into the box after she had transferred to the driver's seat. Karen soon became adept at "jumping" across from her wheelchair into the driver's seat, bringing the hoist down from the rooftop box using specially provided controls, folding her wheelchair and hooking it onto the hoist, then pushing another button to take her wheelchair up onto the car's roof and into the weather-proof box. It is no exaggeration to say that this car completely changed Karen's life. She was now independently mobile and there was a world out there to explore.

By September of 1984, Michael, now eleven-years old, had left Booker Avenue school behind and started his secondary education at Calderstones Comprehensive, formerly my alma mater, Quarry Bank High School, which held many happy memories for me. The gradual replacement of grammar schools by non-selective comprehensive schools during the late 1960s and early 1970s was a backward step as far as I was concerned. The perceived wisdom of the day was that the grammar school system favoured the rich but I came from one of the poorest areas of Liverpool and still went to one of the best grammar schools in the country.

During the summer of 1985, our faithful golden Labrador, Sandy, was ten-years-old and approaching the end of her life. We decided to get another dog to soften the blow when Sandy eventually died and went to see a local Labrador breeder. We allowed our twelve-year-old son, Michael, to choose from the litter and he chose a six-week-old black Labrador bitch. He immediately christened her "Smokie" and the latest addition to our family slept on Michael's lap as we drove home.

When we introduced Smokie to Sandy, the young pup tormented her by constantly nipping her with her sharp baby teeth. Sandy took this in her stride and gently pushed Smokie away when her behaviour became too boisterous. Sandy was now an arthritic old lady who was happy to sleep the day away but Smokie wouldn't let her rest. When Sandy went to her own basket for a snooze, Smokie would immediately jump in beside her, nuzzling and nipping. So, Sandy would slowly get up and settle down again in Smokie's basket, only for Smokie to join her and continue the playful harassment of her elder "sister". Poor Sandy couldn't get any peace but she was amazingly tolerant of the young pup and they became inseparable until Sandy died in her sleep two years later with Smokie snuggled up beside her.

A few weeks later, on Saturday 6th July 1985, my business partner and cousin, Brian and his lovely wife, Angela, organised a surprise 40th birthday party for yours truly at Dovedale Towers and I was genuinely gobsmacked when, instead of the small family meal I was expecting, I arrived at the venue to find around 250 friends and family belting out a rousing "Happy Birthday". I was most surprised that Rita, Karen, and Michael had all managed to keep it a secret! It was a wonderful party and great to catch up with old friends and relatives, some of whom I hadn't seen for many years.

A few short weeks later, though, one of our treasured family members, Rita's mum, Tabitha, suddenly passed away, aged 67. Rita's mum was like Rita herself, always putting others first, never thinking of herself, and she would be greatly missed. Nanny Tab, as Karen and Michael called her, was much loved and we were all devastated by her passing. Although wracked with grief, Rita's first thoughts were for her father, Sylvester, who had lost the love of his life. Syl had been a tough sergeant major in the Second World War and he had seen many of his friends die in battle. But dealing with the death of his wife of forty-eight years was truly traumatic. It was also Karen and Michael's first encounter with the death of a close relative and it hurt me to see them both so upset. Rita was, of course, inconsolable. Her mum had been a great friend as well as a loving mother.

Some weeks later, while I was working in London, Rita returned home from her keep-fit class to find Karen on the floor, trapped between the toilet and her wheelchair.

Karen said, "Don't panic, Mum, but when I fell, I heard a loud crack. I thing I have broken my leg."

Sure enough, one of her legs was bent at an unnatural angle. Rita immediately called an ambulance and Karen was taken to the Royal Liverpool Hospital. Her right femur was broken and required an operation to pin it back together. The only good thing was that Karen didn't feel any pain. Again, she showed great resilience and made a quick recovery.

-0-0-0-0-0-

Towards the end of September 1986, my mum, Ann, aged 62, had a minor heart attack and was admitted to the Royal Liverpool hospital. I visited Mum in the Cardiac Unit and she seemed to be recovering well so, directly from the hospital, I drove to London for a particularly important week that would cumulate with a huge testing exercise over the coming weekend. I sent Mum some flowers to let her know I was thinking of her and got stuck into work. The Saturday testing session went well and I hoped that Sunday would be equally successful so that I could return home to Liverpool. However, at around 6:30am on Sunday morning, I was woken by the strident ringing of my phone. It was my brother, Geoff.

"Dave, Mum has had another heart attack and..." his voice cracked. "... this time, her heart stopped altogether. They tried to revive her but..." he couldn't continue.

"I will be home as soon as possible." I managed to say.

"Please don't drive back. Get the train," he said, but I was no longer listening. I hung up, washed and dressed in record time and pointed the car back towards Liverpool for the 200 mile drive up the M1 and onto the M6. At this time, my car was a red Datsun 300ZX sports car and it had a top speed of 175 miles per hour. I don't remember the drive back. I was functioning on auto-pilot. I just kept thinking.... Why did this have to happen on the only weekend I was working in that year? My brothers and sisters and Rita were at Mum's house comforting Dad, who was absolutely distraught. I arrived there at 8:30am, so I guess I was exceeding the speed limit on the almost deserted motorways. Everyone was crying and hugging each other. My beloved mum was dead. I couldn't believe it. She had been a constant in my life for more than 40 years and we would all miss her terribly.

-0-0-0-0-0-

After completing her Business & Administration course at the Greenbank Project in 1986, Karen enrolled at Millbank College to complete a number of Pitman touch-typing courses, which she hoped would help her land a job as a secretary or receptionist. During her time at Millbank, Karen met Caroline Mosses and they immediately became close friends. Two years and several nationally-recognised qualifications later, Karen decided to enrol on a Business Studies course in the same college, which would also enhance her prospects of getting a job. She completed the course and, armed with several diplomas, she was ready to begin her working career.

Her obvious first destination was, of course, Microtech Computer Services, which Brian and I had started in January 1980. The Liverpool office was based in the iconic Cotton Exchange Building in the city centre, which also housed one of the company's IT training centres. Both Brian and I had IT backgrounds and, for a few years we had actually worked together at United Biscuits as computer programmers. Immediately before forming Microtech, Brian was a senior manager at an IT training company, which ran government courses backed by the (then) Manpower Services Commission. At the end of the courses, the aim was to place its graduates into full-time employment in the IT sector.

Given Brian's background, it was not surprising that one of our objectives was to offer similar courses at the first opportunity. Our other main objective was to provide bespoke software for small businesses and, to this end, we bought a standard suite of business accounting programs for sales, purchase, and nominal ledgers, which we believed could be customised to suit any kind of business. The programs were written in the BASIC language, which was Microsoft's first programming language for its fledgling MS-DOS operating system. Brian would focus on sales and I would provide the technical expertise.

We were not immediately successful and for many months we had just two desks in around 2,000 square feet of office space! During this time, I did some consultancy work for companies in Toronto and London, which brought in a little money and one of these companies, a London commodity broker called R J Rouse, subsequently called me in to help them with a major headache. At this time, the administration of their business was completely paper-based and, when they were taken over by a much bigger company, the volume of their business doubled virtually overnight, which meant 16-hour days for their beleaguered clerical staff. Bill Bradwell, Rouse's Financial Director, wanted to computerise his business as quickly as possible and the first job (the solution to the headache!) was to develop an Open Position Valuation system, which would automate the most time-consuming and error-prone manual process. Working with one of Rouse's senior back office staff, Peter Sawyer, who provided the business expertise, I wrote the first release of the software in a couple of weeks and, to cut a long story short, news of this software breakthrough soon got around the City of London, and within a few months, two other commodity brokers had signed up for the software.

Meanwhile, back in Liverpool, Brian was equally busy and soon had a couple of small businesses signed up for the accounting software. He also produced a proposal for the Manpower Services Commission to run a BASIC programming course for unemployed Liverpool school-leavers. We were delighted when the proposal was accepted and soon we had converted some of our empty space in the Cotton Exchange into a classroom for 20+ students. The first course was very successful and this side of our business really took off when we provided similar courses in the Elephant and Castle and Southgate areas of London.

So, in 1989, it was into this busy environment that Karen was introduced. She worked in the office, answering the telephone, typing, filing, and helping with the many administrative tasks associated with a growing IT company. The facilities in the recently-refurbished Cotton Exchange Building were not particularly suitable for a wheelchair user but one entrance was accessible and there were lifts, so Karen could get into the office OK. The toilets, however, presented a problem, as all of the cubicle doors opened inwards and when Karen's wheelchair was close enough to the toilet for her to transfer over, the door wouldn't close. Rita quickly solved this problem by suggesting we hang a curtain across one of the cubicles so Karen could have some measure of privacy.

-0-0-0-0-0-

On Saturday 13th October 1990, Rita and I celebrated our 25th wedding anniversary with a party for around 300 family and friends at Liverpool's flagship Adelphi Hotel, a beautiful Edwardian building in Liverpool's city centre. The party was to be held in the evening in the Adelphi's fabulous ballroom and we were booked into the hotel for the night, before travelling to London to join the Orient Express bound for Venice. Just before 2pm on the day of the party, we were surprised when a limousine arrived and we thought it was really kind of our children to arrange for us to travel to the Adelphi in style. We were already packed and ready to go and gleefully climbed into the luxurious leather interior. Very soon it became obvious we were not going directly to the Adelphi and the driver told us he had to make a quick stop on the way. We arrived at St Michael's Church in Garston, where we were originally married, to find my best man and cousin, Ken Chapman, and Rita's original bridesmaids waiting outside. It seemed that the sneaky Karen and Michael had arranged for us to renew our marriage vows! Ken and I climbed the two flights of steps and entered the church, which was bursting at the seams with our family and friends, most of whom had been present on this day 25 years ago.

Ken and I strolled down the aisle, pausing for occasional handshakes and good wishes, and as we arrived at the altar, the strains of the Wedding March started up, the current Vicar stepped forward, and a tearful Rita, clutching a posy of flowers, walked down the aisle on her father's arm. It was a beautiful service and, when it was over, we stepped outside for photographs, before getting back into the limo which would finally take us to the Adelphi.

The party was a great success. My Dad, Frank, had arranged for the entertainment and acted as compere for the evening's festivities. After a risqué performance by two naked men, who danced while holding a balloon in each hand, constantly switching balloons to cover their private parts, the well-known local comedian, Al Dean, the king of the one-liners, strolled through the packed tables, finding suitable candidates for his vitriolic wit. He approached my nieces, Jacqui and Helen, and asked them if they were sisters. "Yes," they both nodded. "Where's Cinderella?" he asked, deadpan, before moving on to his next victim.

The stars of the show, though, were Faron's Flamingos, a popular Liverpool group from the Merseybeat era of the 1960's, who made a few records, notably "Do You Love Me", which was later covered by Brian Poole and the Tremeloes and became a smash hit. They sang many of the most popular songs of the 60's and finished with a rousing rendition of "Do You Love Me", when Faron dragged me up to sing along with the chorus.

The next morning, nursing hangovers, but still buzzing from the party, Rita and I caught a train to London, took a taxi from Euston to Victoria Station and joined a luxury Pullman service, where we enjoyed a traditional afternoon tea en-route to Dover. After crossing the channel on a fast but noisy hovercraft, we joined the iconic Venice-Simplon Orient Express, which would take us through France into Austria and to the famous Brenner mountain pass, through the Alps, and down into Italy to our final destination, Venice's Santa Lucia station. On board, we enjoyed a four-course dinner in the restaurant car, before retiring to our cabin, which had been converted into a cosy bedroom by our steward. I ordered an early morning call for when we reached the Brenner pass, so we could enjoy the wonderful Alpine scenery, and enjoyed a continental breakfast in our cabin before arriving in Venice around midday.

We were then transported by motor launch to the beautiful Cipriani, one of the world's finest hotels, which is located on its own private island in the Venice lagoon directly across from St Mark's Square. Our room had a complimentary bottle of champagne and a jacuzzi. Heaven! We explored Venice for three days before transferring to the airport for our flight home. This was a truly memorable holiday that we would never forget.

-0-0-0-0-0-

During the latter months of 1990, Karen began to experience pain in her lower back and a subsequent x-ray revealed that one of the surgical screws, which held her metalwork in place, had penetrated a kidney and it was no longer functioning. She was referred to Mr Bell, a renal specialist at Liverpool's Royal Hospital, who recommended the kidney should be removed. The surgery was carried out in December at the same time I was in Lourdes Hospital having my first hip replacement. I was 45 years old and was diagnosed with severe osteo-arthritis in my left hip, apparently due to "wear and tear". My right hip was also showing signs of wear and this would need to be replaced in the not-too-distant future. And I thought exercise was supposed to be good for you!

Karen recovered from her kidney surgery and appeared none-the-worse for the experience. Soon after she returned to work, Brian and I agreed an amicable split of the business. I would take the London-based Financial Systems business, which had expanded considerably in the intervening years, and he would retain the remainder of the business, which was by now predominantly IT training. When there are two equal partners in a business, when one doesn't agree with a particular idea or development, it can lead to friction, so a split was good for both of us.

Karen thoroughly enjoyed working in Microtech's busy Liverpool office but she was less than pleased when Brian asked her to work as the receptionist in a spin-off company, a small local factory printing bespoke computer stationery. She went from a vibrant office environment to a three-person operation and, as a committed "people" person, she missed the office banter and gossip.

Consequently, in 1992, now aged 26, Karen joined Liverpool City Council after seeing an advert in the local newspaper for a secretary/receptionist position, initially based in an office in Liverpool city centre, which had a steep flight of steps at the front of the building.

Obviously, she couldn't get in the front of the building without help, so she parked her car behind the office and used the goods lift to get to her 3rd floor office. Later she transferred to the Moss Grove Family Homeless Service, providing accommodation for homeless families and asylum seekers. Here she met Sandra Ravenhill, who assessed homeless applicants and organised suitable accommodation for genuine cases, and they soon became close friends.

Around this time, Karen started following the English Chippendales, a troupe of male strippers (hey, I never claimed she was an angel!), and she met their manager, Tony James-Gorman, who became another life-long friend. The Chippendales were founded in Los Angeles in the early 1980s by Steve Banerjee, who's dream was to transform male stripping from a drunken hen-night sleaze-fest into a showbiz extravaganza that would attract woman from all backgrounds. The Chippendales certainly attracted Karen, who drove all over the country to their shows. At one of her first shows, she met fellow Chippendale fans, Janine, Irene, and Donna, who soon became close friends with whom she would often share hotel rooms.

In August 1992, Karen ticked off another item on her bucket list when she accompanied Rita and I on a three-day trip to Memphis, Tennessee, which included a tour of Graceland, the home and final resting place of her idol, Elvis Presley. We explored Elvis's living quarters, including the famous Jungle Room, and ended the tour in the Meditation Garden, where Elvis and his close family were laid to rest.

Later, we explored the historic Beale Street, the acknowledged "Home of the Blues", with its range of restaurants and blues clubs, including the Jerry Lee Lewis Café & Honky Tonk and B. B. King's Blues Club, and moved on to tour the Sun Recording Studios, where the eighteen-year-old Elvis, fresh from graduating high school, recorded his first songs, *My Happiness* and *That's When Your Heartaches Begin* in August 1953. The studio is also famous for hosting an impromptu jam session in December 1956, featuring Elvis Presley, Jerry Lee Lewis, Carl Perkins, and Johnny Cash, who were all trying to make their way in the music business. The rest, as they say, is history!

From Memphis, we moved on to Los Angeles, where we visited the up-market designer shops on Rodeo Drive, the glamourous Hollywood Walk of Fame, the iconic Sunset Boulevard, Santa Monica Pier with its Ferris Wheel and fairground attractions, and the down-to-earth Farmers' Market.

Unfortunately, an urgent business problem meant I had to cut my holiday short and I flew back to London, leaving Rita and Karen to enjoy LA without me. Running your own business is not all it's cracked up to be, believe me. I was truly pissed off and the first seeds of doubt were sown. I had always wanted to run my own business but my advice to would-be entrepreneurs is – be careful what you wish for.

-0-0-0-0-0-

In June 1993, in a period when the UK economy was suffering from a downturn, I decided to sell my financial software business. At this time, the London office housed around 25 employees, many of whom were highly-paid technicians and the Sydney office, led by my brother Barry, who had emigrated to Australia some years earlier, accommodated another 6 employees. In recent months, meeting the monthly payroll had become a regular struggle, increasing my stress levels accordingly.

Unfortunately, the company's business model resulted in periods of feast and famine. In buoyant times, financial services companies spent huge sums on software but, in recession, they spent next to nothing. I wanted to change the company's business model from one based on a one-off, lifetime software licence, which cost from £50,000 up to £500,000, depending on the number of users, to a monthly licence fee, which would provide regular monthly income and even-out the current cash flow peaks and troughs. However, when I did the maths, I realised I would need to raise around £750,000 to cover costs during the transition period. Reluctantly, because in good times, the company was very profitable, I decided to cut my losses and started looking for a buyer.

The companies I spoke to didn't like the company's current business model either, but they were very interested in the financial software, which had been developed over many years. I eventually agreed a deal with SunGard, an American-owned multi-national providing software and services to the global financial services sector. Basically, SunGard agreed to buy the rights to the software and the considerable user base, after which I would wind up the company. They also agreed to take on all of the staff who wanted to transfer over to their company, except for me, who was tied to a non-competition clause, preventing me from working in a competing financial software company for three years. In return, during this non-compete period, they paid me a monthly consultancy fee. Ostensibly, they could call on me at any time but, after the first six months, they rarely called, which suited me just fine. The only part of the deal that I didn't like was that SunGard were not interested in taking on Barry and his staff, as they already had a fully-staffed Sydney office. I was distressed to learn that Barry struggled for some time after this setback but, fortunately, the cream always rises to the top and, with two close friends, he eventually started his own highly-successful software consultancy business. Good on yer, mate!

-0-0-0-0-0-

After being in the IT industry for almost thirty years, in 1993, I made a disastrous foray into the wholesale marble and granite business. A close friend of mine, Peter Barton, who had his own memorials business, mentioned that his gravestone supplier, J A Emsley & Sons, based in Liverpool, was for sale. One of the founder's sons, Mick Emsley, currently ran the business but he was stricken with terminal cancer and wanted to sell the business before he passed on. The business had once been profitable but, largely due to Mick's ill-health, it was currently floundering. It sounded like a challenge, though, and one that Peter and I were willing to take on.

We agreed a deal with Mick and I took over as Managing Director. There was very little stock in the yard at this time and we invested a considerable amount of money in buying new stocks of marble and granite from suppliers in Italy and India. Peter and I travelled to Carrara in Italy to meet the company's long-time white marble supplier in the hope of continuing the excellent relationship that Mick had originally established.

With regular supplies re-established, we then had to focus on increasing sales. I brought Michael into the company to work in the yard as a labourer while he got to know the business, after which he would become a full-time salesman, visiting old and new clients to stimulate sales.

By the summer of 1994, Michael was twenty-one years-old and had already, two years previously, met his future wife, Joanne Tate, on a Mediterranean holiday to the island of Rhodes. He and Joanne were now settled in their own Liverpool flat with Archie, their ginger-tom cat. Joanne was actually from the north east of England, from a small village located between Durham and Sunderland but, when she met Michael, she was living and working in Blackpool, a 100-mile round-trip from Liverpool. It wasn't long, though, before she moved to Liverpool to be with Michael. Joanne also joined the Emsley business and was a great help to me in the office.

Slowly but surely, over a period of more than a year, sales began to increase and, after visiting a number of quarries in India, we started to offer many other varieties of granite, in addition to the ubiquitous black granite. By this time, Mick Emsley had unfortunately passed away and part of our deal with him was to pay his wife a monthly sum out of the business. This was a huge strain on the company's finances at a time when investment to grow the business was required. I approached Mrs Emsley and asked could we suspend payments for three months, which she kindly agreed to. However, three months became six months and Mrs Emsley lost patience and eventually, with no warning, she called in the receivers. Had she spoken to me first, I am sure we could have worked something out but, within weeks, the receiver had sold off the company's stock and other assets at a fraction of their true value to pay Mrs Emsley what she was owed and the company was forced into liquidation. This experience cost Peter and I a great deal of time, effort, and money. The best business advice I was ever given was "Stick to what you know!". If only I had remembered that before agreeing to take on J A Emsley & Sons!

Seventeen

After the Emsley debacle, I belatedly took note of the great business advice I failed to heed and offered my services as a Financial Markets Software Consultant to the City of London's famous Square Mile, via a specialist employment agency. To my surprise, within a few days, I was asked to attend an interview at Credit Lyonnais Rouse, a leading French bank and, to my further surprise, the guy I was scheduled to meet was Bill Bradwell, the ex-Financial Director of R J Rouse, who gave me a start in financial markets software all those years ago. Bill was now the Managing Director of Credit Lyonnais Rouse and the original company had been taken over first by Mercantile House and then Credit Lyonnais.

I travelled to London to meet with Bill and after a very short interview, more like a chat really, we agreed a three-year consultancy contract. My brief was to investigate all of the bank's existing computer systems and suggest ways they could be improved using the latest technologies, which included touch-screens (very new at this time) and voice-recognition systems. I was back where I felt I belonged.

The downside was being away from my family during the working week but the generous monthly consultancy fee was too good to turn down. I soon rented a nice ground-floor flat in the Winchmore Hill area, where a number of my old friends from the Microtech days lived. The weekly commute was arduous but I could put up with it for three years.

When the Emsley business folded, Joanne went on to study Fashion & Design at Liverpool Community College and, after graduating, she became a Fashion & Design tutor at the Greenbank Project. Meanwhile, Michael, along with my Dad, worked in the Special Memories memorial shop in the affluent Allerton Road area, which I had set up during the Emsley years. Mike and Joanne also lived in the flat above the shop. Life went on.

Karen still lived at home with Rita and I, enjoying a busy life-style with no further medical complications to concern us. She worked from Monday to Friday and, like most young single women, on the weekend, she enjoyed Liverpool city centre's night life. Along with her great friend, Debbie Jones, she would go to her favourite night clubs, bantering with the bouncers and persuading them to carry her and Debbie and their wheelchairs up or down any stairs they may encounter. Karen and Debbie became well known on the Liverpool night club circuit. They were on first name terms with all of the bouncers, who made sure they were well protected whenever the going got a bit rough.

By this time, Smokie was almost twelve-years-old and one sad morning she experienced a stroke, which paralysed her back legs. It was pitiful to see her dragging her hind legs behind her as she tried to move around. Rita and I took her to the local vet and he confirmed that Smokie had suffered a stroke, telling us that the humane thing to do would be to put her to sleep. We had to agree and, with Rita and I beside her, gently cradling her head, the vet administered the fatal injection and, in an instant, Smokie was gone.

-0-0-0-0-0-

By the summer of 1995, Rita's Dad, Sylvester – the war-hero who was so reluctant to speak of his exploits – had been living with us in our Melbreck Road bungalow for a number of years. After he lost his beloved wife, Tabitha, Syl moved out of the family home in Canterbury Street, Garston, and into a small, one-bedroomed flat in Holly Park, once the home of the South Liverpool football team. As his health started to deteriorate, Rita asked him to move in with us so that he could get the help he needed. He moved into Karen's old bedroom, which had an en-suite bathroom, and the front lounge became his personal space, with his own furniture and personal items, including his treasured family photographs.

At this time, Rita and I had a caravan in a holiday park in the North Wales town of Conwy, which we visited almost every weekend. Returning home one Sunday evening, we were met by Rita's eldest sister, Betty, to learn that Syl had apparently had a stroke and could not stand. We immediately called an ambulance and he was taken to Liverpool's Broadgreen hospital.

As he started to recuperate from his stroke, Syl began to hallucinate, regressing to his war years, believing he had been captured by the enemy and the nurses were his guards. Sadly, he passed away on 25 June 1996, aged 80. Rita, who had been his primary carer for the past few years, was grief-stricken and would miss him dearly.

-0-0-0-0-0-

After a mostly enjoyable stint working in the City of London, after three years, I was ready to come home. In 1997, the Internet and the Web were still in their infancy and Internet connection technology relied on very slow modem devices. However, this technology was developing at a fast pace and it was clear to me that more and more businesses would want to establish a web presence. I decided to take some time off to write a book on website development, which I hoped to get published.

However, when the book was almost complete, I realised that it would be better presented as a training course and, as I intended to provide technical support, I could charge a lot more money for it. The WebMaster Web Design training programme was born in a back room of the Special Memories shop. I placed an advertisement in the Daily Mail careers section and the phone started to ring. I printed off a master copy of the course, made numerous photocopies, and inserted them into ring-binders. As the orders began to roll in, I started writing a more advanced follow-up course, which was also successful, many students ordering the two courses as a special offer bundle.

The success of this venture led to the formation of a new family business, Visual Software Training. I closed down Special Memories, rented a large office above a row of shops, and we were in business again, with Rita, Mike, and my Dad all lending a hand.

Visual Software began to prosper when the government introduced a training scheme, Individual Learning Accounts, where any British subject over the age of sixteen could apply for a £200 grant towards the purchase of an accredited training course. We successfully registered for the scheme and began to advertise free web design training for qualifying applicants, which would be funded by the ILA scheme. Orders poured in and the company appeared set for a profitable future.

Unfortunately, the scheme was beset by criminal activity with doorstep con-men, organised gangs of fraudsters, and high-tech computer criminals contributing to the theft of public funds by "harvesting" names and addresses of British citizens and setting up ILA accounts without their knowledge. Law abiding companies like Visual Software were apparently in the minority and the government was forced to close down the scheme after a single fraud, involving the setting up of 80,000 bogus accounts, resulted in the misappropriation of more than £16million! The fraudsters went to prison for long stretches.

-0-0-0-0-0-

In May 1998, Karen, together with her friend and colleague, Sandra, travelled to Los Angeles for a well-deserved holiday. Karen's friends, Angela (Angie) and Mark Donougher, lived in LA at this time as did Angela's sister, Barbara, known as Barbie. Angie and Barbie were Debbie Jones's sisters, so this was going to be a reunion as well as a holiday.

Their hotel was close to the famous Sunset Boulevard and they spent a number of memorable evenings in Sunset's heaving blues clubs. They met up with Angie and Mark whenever they were free but both were working at this time, so only the weekends and the odd evening were available for catching up. It transpired that Barbie was due to marry her fiancé, Clarence, on the 15th May, so Karen and Sandra were invited to attend the wedding ceremony and the following celebration.

On a day when rain was forecast in LA for the first time in more than 40 years at this time of year, Karen and Sandra decided to hire a car and drive to Las Vegas, 270 miles and a 4 to 5-hour ride away on Interstate 15, much of it through the stark, flat landscape of the Mojave Desert. They tuned in to a local popular music station and, windows down, they sang along to the latest releases, including Dance the Night Away by the Mavericks and Let Me Entertain You by Robbie Williams. Hot and sticky, they arrived in Vegas at around 2pm and were soon driving down the vibrant Strip, from the pyramid-shaped Luxor hotel at one end, past the famous Caesar's Palace, MGM Grand, and Mirage hotels, and four miles down to the newly-opened Stratosphere with its near 1,150ft high tower, containing the world's highest roller coaster.

Coincidentally, (hmm, I wonder?) one of Karen's Chippendale dancer friends was performing in a show in one of the big hotels, so they bought tickets and saw the afternoon performance. Needless to say, they had a great time in Vegas, spending time in a number of casinos, playing the slots, hoping to hit the $1,000,000 jackpot.

As darkness fell and the Las Vegas Strip was lit up like no other place on earth, they (reluctantly) left it behind and began the long drive back through the Mojave Desert. The Vegas illuminations, including a laser beam, which sliced through the atmosphere from the top of the Luxor hotel to the edge of space, were visible through Sandra's rear-view mirror for many miles into the black desert night. Five hours later they were safely back at their hotel, tired but exhilarated.

On 15th May, Barbie and Clarence tied the knot during a quiet civil ceremony in a Los Angeles County Registry Office and, after the formalities were completed, the wedding party decamped to a Mexican restaurant and then went on to the Farmers Market bar to celebrate the marriage with a few too many drinks!

Before leaving for home, Karen and Sandra went for a drink in the bar of the Beverly Wilshire hotel, where the film Pretty Woman, starring Richard Gere and Julia Roberts, was mostly shot. They drank Pretty Woman cocktails while people-watching through the picture windows facing Rodeo

Drive. Later, probably due to the strong alcohol content of the cocktails, they had matching, non-permanent, henna designs tattooed on their arms.

I almost forgot to mention that, thanks to Angie, whose friend worked on the show, they were also part of the audience for an episode of the US version of The Price Is Right, the longest-running game show in television history, hosted by Bob Barker for thirty-five years.

-o-o-o-o-o-

Several months before her LA trip, Karen had applied for a purpose-built housing association flat, which was under construction at Little Parkfield Road, close to Lark Lane and its lively bars and restaurants, and she was ecstatic when her application was approved. We were delighted for her, as yet another personal ambition would soon be within her reach.

The one-bedroomed, ground-floor flat, which had been customised to Karen's precise requirements, included a lounge/kitchen with lower than usual counter tops and cupboards, a bathroom with rails to help her transfer to the toilet, and a "roll-in" shower. In June 1998, it was finally ready for occupation and it was a proud moment for all of us when she moved in. Of course, Rita and I helped Karen to decorate and furnish her flat and, within a month or so, she was nicely settled in to her own place, the walls of her flat covered with photographs of her friends and family. For the first time in her life, she was truly independent, with her own flat, a car, and a job.

Karen loved her job at the Moss Grove Family Homeless Service but, although the office was on the ground floor and had a ramp leading to the entrance, she found the toilets difficult to manage. Over a period of time, the additional time it took Karen to take care of business in the toilet led to one colleague, who shall remain nameless, making snide remarks on the lines that Karen spent more time in the toilet than she spent at her desk. I would love for this ignorant woman to spend one day in Karen's shoes and see how she would cope.

Also, we were unaware at this time that Karen was suffering from the onset of rheumatoid arthritis, which was to severely affect the movement of her hands, arms, and shoulders, and which, of course, she relied on to transfer back and forth from her wheelchair to the toilet. Little wonder it was taking longer than usual.

This form of bullying continued until it became so stressful that Karen could no longer face going to the office. Her GP signed her off work for three months, citing depression brought on by work-related stress, during which time Karen decided she couldn't go back while this woman worked there. However, she refused to make a formal complaint and would prefer to simply give up her job, which she did in 2001. Rita and I were, of course, furious and Rita, in particular, wanted to confront this person, but Karen persuaded her to let it lie.

On a happier note, in May 2000, Karen and Sandra visited New York, staying in a hotel in Times Square. Sandra, who takes no crap from anyone, complained that the room wasn't suitable for a wheelchair user and they were subsequently upgraded to a suite free-of-charge! At this time, my old friend, Frank Gilligan, from our United Biscuits days, lived and worked in Manhattan and he took it upon himself to show the ladies around town, not just to the tourist landmarks, such as the Statue of Liberty and the Empire State Building, but to less well-known places like the Champagne & Oyster Bar in Grand Central Station and the numerous Irish bars that were Frank's natural habitat. The trip was a roaring success and Frank later told me that it was his great pleasure to meet Karen and Sandra and to show them around his town.

-0-0-0-0-0-

A year later, in May 2001, Karen, Rita, and I visited Karen's friend, Caroline, who was now Caroline Allsopp, happily married, and living in Cardiff. The occasion was the FA Cup Final between Liverpool and Arsenal, which was to take place at Cardiff's Millennium Stadium while the old Wembley Stadium was being rebuilt. This was the first time that the FA Cup Final had ever been held outside England.

We drove to Cardiff, accompanied by my dad, and arrived at Caroline's place around lunch-time. We stayed for an hour or so before taking a taxi to the stadium. To be fair, Arsenal dominated the game and deservedly took the lead in the 72nd minute. However, two late goals from Michael Owen won the cup for Liverpool to clinch the second of a fabulous treble for Liverpool, who had won the League Cup in February, and would go on to win the EUFA Cup four days after winning the FA Cup. We arrived back at Caroline's house, deliriously happy, and Caroline accompanied us to the lively Cardiff Bay area to celebrate with a meal and several drinks!

Four days later, we were in Dortmund for the EUFA Cup Final against the Spanish team, Alaves. This time, Michael and Joanne were with us. The match finished 4-4 and, in extra time, Liverpool scored the so-called "golden" goal to win the match. The goal was actually scored by one of the Alaves defenders but who cared about that? A historic treble of trophies had been won!

-0-0-0-0-0-

I was just finishing a late lunch on Tuesday 11th September 2001 while watching Countdown, Channel 4's anagrams and numbers game show, when a news flash interrupted the programme – an aeroplane had flown into the North Tower of the World Trade Center in New York City. My first assumption was that a light aircraft had somehow got into difficulties and crashed into one of the world-famous towers but, as more news filtered through, it turned out that the hijacked American Airlines flight 11 – Boston to Los Angeles – had been deliberately flown into the tower by al-Qaeda terrorists, instantly killing all 92 people on board. When the Boeing 767 hit the tower between the 93rd and 99th floors, the jet was travelling at more than 460 miles per hour and was carrying an almost full load of 10,000 gallons of jet fuel with catastrophic consequences.

I immediately tuned in to the BBC 24-hour news channel, which was now showing live pictures of the incident. Approximately 17 minutes after the North Tower was hit, another Boeing 767, United Airlines Flight 175, also en route to Los Angeles from Boston, was deliberately flown into the South Tower by another group of al-Qaeda terrorists. This outrage was captured by television cameras and I would be haunted for weeks afterwards with images of the hijacked plane slicing into the tower followed by a cataclysmic explosion. On live TV, almost an hour after the crash, millions of viewers from around the world saw the South Tower collapse in a gigantic cloud of dust. The North Tower suffered a similar fate around 15 minutes later and the whole of Lower Manhattan was shrouded in grey dust with a vast empty space where the instantly-recognisable twin towers had one proudly stood.

My first thought was for my old mate, Frank Gilligan, who worked in the World Trade Center. I rang his home number, not expecting to get through, but anxious to know if he was OK, and was hugely relieved when he answered. Lucky for Frank, he was working from home on that fateful day. My second thought was that I could have been caught up in this disaster. Two weeks earlier I had been in the 100th floor North Tower offices of the financial services group of the giant AON insurance company for a meeting regarding a potential business venture, where I was acting as an IT consultant for a New York City company called Pacer Power. AON lost 176 employees who had all been working on the 100th floor on the day of the terrorist attacks, including the guys I had been meeting with. There but for the grace of God…

-0-0-0-0-0-

Rita and I were determined to allow Karen to see as much of the world as possible while her health lasted and, with this in mind, on the day before Christmas Eve, 2001, Rita, Karen, and I flew from Manchester Airport to Singapore in style, enjoying Singapore Airlines' excellent Business Class and staying at the 5-star Mandarin Oriental hotel on Marina Bay for three nights, before flying on to Sydney to enjoy New Year with my brother Barry and his wife, Angela.

Christian Singaporeans traditionally celebrate Christmas with a lavish party on Christmas Eve, on a par with our New Year's Eve celebrations, so it was a little strange having Christmas "lunch" with all the trimmings on Christmas Eve at the Mandarin in the sultry heat of Singapore. It was even stranger having a Burger King for lunch on Christmas Day, but Rita and Karen enjoyed the great shopping on offer in the air-conditioned malls of Orchard Road, before we moved on to the famous Raffles Hotel, where we each enjoyed a Singapore Sling cocktail in the Long Bar.

In Sydney, it was great to catch up with Barry and Angela and, on New Year's Eve, which is also Barry's birthday, we all went to a music festival at Hyde Park, the oldest public park in Australia, from where we had a grandstand view of the amazing Harbour Bridge fireworks display at midnight.

-0-0-0-0-0-

One Friday evening in early June, 2002, I returned home from work to find Rita crying softly in the kitchen of our Melbreck Road bungalow. Two weeks earlier we had agreed to the sale of our family home, which was now too big for just the two of us, after both Karen and Michael had flown the nest. That afternoon, Rita had retrieved several cardboard boxes from the loft, where they had lain since the day we first occupied the house more than twenty-seven years earlier. Rita sat on a high stool at the breakfast bar. A faded greeting card lay open in front of her on the steel-blue surface.

'What's the matter, sweetheart?' I asked, kissing her cheek, tasting the salt of her tears. Rita closed the card and handed it to me without replying. Printed on the card, in an attractive, cursive script, was the legend:

To My Darling Wife on the Birth of Our Baby

The word 'Baby' was printed in a larger font than the remainder of the message, and inside the extra-large letter 'B' was a picture of a baby girl, sleeping with a thumb between her pink rosebud lips. I opened the card and read a message printed in the same curling font.

It's wonderful to have a Wife, As dear and sweet as You

And such a joy to welcome, Our precious Baby, too…

And so with all my love I send, this message, dear, to say

God bless you both and keep you, Ever happy on Life's way

Underneath the verse, I recognised my own handwriting, marginally different to my writing today, but still familiar more than thirty-six years after the original was written. The ink had faded over the years, but the message was clearly visible:

To my darling wife, Rio, on the birth of our daughter, Karen.

Hoping you and Baby Karen regain your health as soon as possible.

May the years ahead be full of sunshine and happiness for both of you,

Your loving husband, Dave.

xxxxxx

Where had those 36 years gone?

Eighteen

By the middle of July 2002, Rita and I had moved to a ground-floor apartment in Birkdale, close to the famous Royal Birkdale links golf course, and we had only been there a few weeks when Karen suffered her first rheumatoid arthritis episode. It happened while I was in Southport & Formby District General Hospital, suffering from a form of cardiomyopathy, apparently triggered by a virus attacking my heart and causing irreparable muscle damage. Karen phoned Rita and told her she was in agony and couldn't get herself out of bed. Rita raced to Karen's flat and helped her out of bed, before making an appointment with her GP, Dr Brookes, who quickly referred her to rheumatoid specialist, Dr Bucknall, at the Royal Liverpool Hospital.

Rheumatoid arthritis is a long-term condition that causes pain, swelling and stiffness in the joints and, in Karen's case, it was her hands, arms, and shoulders that were affected. Sufferers experience periods, known as flare-ups, where symptoms become much worse. Flare-ups are difficult to predict but with medication, Dr Bucknall advised Karen that it was possible to substantially decrease their frequency. As it turned out, Karen's rheumatoid arthritis effectively ended her working career.

As for my cardiomyopathy, I had been experiencing acute shortage of breath for a number of months and, during the first few days in hospital, my cardiologist told me that, if the medication he was prescribing did not improve my condition, I would need a heart transplant! Fortunately, after a week of intense medication, I started to feel better and no longer required supplementary oxygen to breath. I was then discharged from hospital and referred to a cardiologist for follow-up treatment. My days of rigorous exercise were over and I was unable to work for a period of two years while my heart recovered. It would never become 100% functional again but I hoped my heart would learn to cope without the muscle destroyed by the virus.

To make matters worse, the arthritis in my right hip was now very painful and my GP arranged for me to see an orthopaedic specialist at Southport & Formby District General Hospital. His name was Mr Ali and, after checking over my notes, he pompously declared that I was "decrepit" (yes, really!) and categorically refused to take the risk of operating on me because of my heart condition. An utterly charming man was Mr Ali.

At this time, Michael and Joanne were planning on starting a family and, understandably, Joanne wanted her children to be raised in the relatively quiet rural environment of her home village in the north east of England. By this time, they were living in their own house in Mossley Hill, close to the bars and restaurants of Rose Lane and Allerton Road. As it happened, Rita and I could not settle in Birkdale, which was twenty-five miles from Karen's flat, so we agreed to buy their house to facilitate their move to the north east.

-0-0-0-0-0-

During this enforced period of relative inactivity, I decided to take a Creative Writing course at the University of Liverpool and, subsequently, began to write this story. I was still in a lot of pain with my arthritic right hip and my Liverpool GP referred me to the surgeon who replaced my left hip back in 1990, Mr Thompson, at the Royal Hospital. He asked his close colleague, Dr Jane Beattie, a Consultant Anaesthetist, to check me over and, God bless her, she didn't find me at all "decrepit". Mr Thompson, assisted by Dr Beattie, successfully replaced my hip in 1993. The operation was routine and five days later I walked out of the hospital on crutches – pain free.

After two years of recuperation, my heart had recovered as much as it was ever going to and I was ready to start work again. There were virtually no opportunities in the financial systems sector in Liverpool so I had to take what I could get and joined St Helens Glass as a freelance conservatory salesman. However, after a few months, Rob Lowry, an old friend, who was my second-in-command at Microtech Financial Systems, called me and asked if I was interested in six months work at the company he had founded with three more of my ex-employees at Microtech. He invited me to London to discuss this opportunity and we had a chat over lunch.

Many years earlier, Rob had successfully completed a Microtech programming training course in Liverpool and I subsequently found him a job in London, before he joined me at Microtech when the commodity broking business started to take off. He told me that his company, Exchange Systems Technology, had recently won a contract with J P Morgan Chase Bank, a leading global financial institution based in Bournemouth, and he needed someone to write a detailed functional specification as part of the contract. Was I interested? Damn right I was and, within a couple of weeks, I was back in the game! Working out of Exchange Systems' City Road office, I rented a flat in Winchmore Hill, and it soon seemed like I had never been away.

After a few months and with good progress being made on the J P Morgan project, Rob offered me a permanent job as a Senior Business Analyst. Rita and I discussed the offer and, as always, she supported me 100% in whatever decision I made. It was nigh on impossible to earn the sort of salary I had been offered in Liverpool, so I accepted the position and began the familiar Liverpool to London commute, catching an early train to London on Monday morning and making the return journey late afternoon on Friday. I expected this situation to last for a couple of years at most but, little did I know, it would be a further ten years before I eventually severed my ties with the City of London.

In 2003, Michael took over the bare bones of Visual Software Training to focus on the e-learning (online learning) sector, quickly establishing a number of partnerships with other course providers. He created a vibrant new website, branded as Distance Learning Centre, offering a wide range of courses on subjects as diverse as gardening and psychology as well as the web design courses I had originally written. I wished him well, of course, but even I was surprised at how successful his new venture ultimately became. He turned out to be an astute businessman and carefully managed the growth of his business without the need for a bank overdraft. He paid his bills promptly, was popular with suppliers and customers alike, and Rita and I were extremely proud of him.

-0-0-0-0-0-

To our great delight, on 2nd February 2006, Michael and Joanne's first son, Joseph, our first grandson, was born. Even at a few days old, it was clear that he favoured the Tate side of the family, looking like a mini Grandad Peter! Karen was thrilled by the new addition to our family and it brought tears to my eyes to see baby Joseph cradled in her arms. She craved to be a mother herself but, by this time, I think she was resigned to being the best Auntie she could possibly be.

In the first week of May 2006, a few days before Karen's forthcoming 40th birthday party, she began to experience occasional headaches, blackouts, and convulsions, classic signs that her shunt valve was not working as it should. A long time had gone by since the current shunt was inserted, so long in fact that we forgot how bad the symptoms were when it was blocked. These episodes only lasted a few minutes and then Karen would be back to normal again for days at a time.

Even though she was unwell, Karen did not want to cancel her birthday party, as she cherished the times when all of her friends and family were together. However, Karen's mood was subdued. She complained of a headache but, fortunately, she experienced no further symptoms during the party. However, soon after, she was referred to her neurosurgeon, Conor Malucci, at Aintree Hospital's neurological unit, the Walton Centre.

After a skull x-ray and MRI scan, Mr Malucci immediately suspected Karen's shunt was blocked and, as we had thought, it would have to be replaced. After some deliberation, he suggested that he would insert another shunt on the opposite side of her skull, rather than take the old one out and replace it. He also told us that, if the new shunt didn't stop Karen's symptoms, a more drastic chiari operation would be required.

"The chiari procedure involves removing a small piece of bone from the base of the skull and another bone from the top of the spine, relieving pressure on the brainstem and spinal cord and restoring the normal flow of cerebro-spinal fluid." he said. "This is a major operation and, as part of the post-operative care, the patient has a metal frame attached to the skull to prevent the head from moving."

Karen sat with her head bowed and Rita and I exchanged worried looks.

He continued, "We will admit Karen immediately and schedule the shunt operation for tomorrow."

After a short wait, a porter arrived to take us to the ward. Here, the ward sister told us that the chiari operation was a serious procedure and she urged us to think very carefully before agreeing to it, She said that, in all probability, after the operation, Karen's neck would be fused and that she would need to twist her shoulders to turn her head.

To pass the time, Karen, Rita, and I played Pontoon and, during one game, Karen became unresponsive, staring fixedly ahead. We shouted for help and Karen started to convulse. Two nurses ran to her, lifted her out of her wheelchair, and lay her in the recovery position on her bed. As you might imagine, this is very distressing. Fortunately, the episode only lasted a couple of minutes and Karen soon came around.

In the next bed to Karen was a young lady called Laura Tyndall, who had a brain tumour and was waiting for an operation to remove it. Karen and Laura were soon chatting like old friends.

Karen's shunt operation took place the following day and, when she returned to the ward, Karen looked much better, even with her head swathed in bandages. After sleeping off the anaesthetic, she was back to her old self and Mr Malucci confirmed later that the old shunt valve was "the worse for wear" after so many years but the new one was working perfectly. The chiari procedure was not mentioned again, much to our relief.

Laura had her operation the same day and, thankfully, her brain tumour was successfully removed and she was expected to make a full recovery. Karen was soon discharged from hospital, but not before exchanging contact details with Laura, and returned to her flat with no apparent ill-effects. Laura, of course, became another great friend.

-0-0-0-0-0-

In June of 2008, the year that Liverpool was awarded the prestigious European Capital of Culture accolade, we accompanied Karen on her first cruising holiday on board the MV Thomson Celebration. Rita and I had previously been on a Caribbean cruise onboard P&O's Oceana and we absolutely loved the whole experience, visiting a new port almost every day. For Karen's debut cruise, we flew to the Cretan capital, Heraklion, and joined the Celebration for a week's tour of the eastern Mediterranean, calling at Corfu Town, Piraeus (for the ancient monuments of Athens), the island of Kefalonia, famous as the setting for the film, Captain Corelli's Mandolin, the beautiful, but battle-scarred, Croatian port of Dubrovnik, and the wonderful Italian city of Venice and its renowned canals and gondolas.

This was just the start of many cruise holidays. We particularly enjoyed P&O's luxurious Ventura, Azura, and Britannia ships. P&O's disabled cabins were perfect for Karen, with bars to help her transfer to the toilet and a large roll-in shower. On board a cruise ship, Karen was almost totally independent. Nearly every part of the ship was accessible to her and she would often go exploring on her own, usually ending up in the ship's casino! We visited the western and eastern Mediterranean on numerous occasions, the lovely island of Madeira, the Canary Islands, the Baltic ports, including an overnight stay in St Petersburg and its fabulous Winter Palace, the former residence of a succession of Russian Tsars.

As soon as we returned from one cruise holiday, Karen would be avidly looking forward to the next one, meticulously researching the ports of call, checking if they were wheelchair-friendly and planning the places she would like to visit.

-0-0-0-0-0-

On April 4th 2009, our second grandson, Ben, was born. Unlike Joseph, Ben looked just like his dad. Rita and I doted on our grandsons, as did their Auntie Karen, and, although they lived 165 miles from Liverpool, we tried to visit them every four weeks or so. By this time, Karen's transport was a converted Ford Transit van, with hand controls and a tail lift. The driver's seat was electrically operated and almost infinitely adjustable. It could be swung around so that Karen could transfer easily from her wheelchair and she could then swing it back around to its normal driving position at the flick of a switch. It could also be electrically raised and lowered and moved forward and back. The van was invaluable, especially when we were travelling to Southampton to join a cruise ship, loaded down with luggage and a spare wheelchair.

Just as their father had when he was a youngster, both Joseph and Ben accepted Karen and her wheelchair without question. When Joseph was three, he asked his Auntie Karen to go upstairs to play in his bedroom, but was satisfied with Karen's reply that she had "sore legs" and couldn't walk. He never asked again. He simply accepted that he had to play with Auntie Karen downstairs.

As Karen's rheumatoid arthritis became more debilitating, she needed an electric wheelchair to move around her flat and she especially needed it for shopping trips. She became a familiar figure whizzing around Speke Retail Park in her "lecky" chair on Friday afternoons after a visit to the hairdressers with her Mum.

Concerned that her arm muscles would deteriorate through lack of use, we bought a set of power-assisted wheels that could be fitted to Karen's manual wheelchair. With the E-Motion wheels fitted, only a small amount of effort was required to self-propel the chair. This meant that Karen could get some much-needed exercise and would be less reliant on her electric wheelchair.

Nineteen

In the autumn of 2010, I began to get occasional, but excruciating, pain in the left hip that had been replaced twenty years earlier. The pain was caused by the implant starting to loosen inside the top of my femur. Certain movements would cause the implant to move and grate against the bone. My GP referred me to an orthopaedic trauma surgeon, Mr Colin Dunlop, who was based at the private Spire Hospital, which was covered by my private health insurance.

I had the operation on 20th December and enjoyed the Spire Christmas lunch along with Rita and Karen. Not a great way to spend Christmas Day but I was discharged a few days later. Mr Dunlop, who was soon to transfer to Jersey, saw me off with the words "Don't worry. This hip will last you a lifetime." – words that would prove less than prophetic.

-0-0-0-0-0-

At this time, Rita continued to visit Karen in her flat almost every day and it broke her heart to see Karen's condition deteriorating. Karen now struggled to transfer to and from the toilet without Rita's help and we discussed how we could make this easier for her.

"The problem is that Karen can no longer "jump" the gap between the toilet and the wheelchair," Rita told me one Saturday morning. "If we had a sort of open-ended wooden box we could slip over one of the wheelchair foot rests, bridging the gap, then she could slide onto the box and then onto the toilet. Do you think you could make something, Dave?"

"I don't see why not," I replied. "We can go down to the flat later, put the wheelchair next to the toilet, take some measurements, get some strong plywood from B&Q, and see what we can do."

At the flat, Rita was able to show me exactly what she had in mind. We needed a wooden box with no bottom and no front that was strong enough to support Karen's weight. Rita suggested we cover it in sheepskin to provide some padding and comfort.

Off I went to B&Q, picked up a sheet of half-inch plywood and asked the guy who operated the circular saw to saw it into four pieces to the precise sizes I had previously measured. I also picked up some angle brackets to strengthen the joints and I was good to go.

Back at home, I glued and screwed the pieces together, placed the structure on the floor, stood on it, jumped on it, and pronounced it strong enough to support Karen's weight. I then chamfered the sharp edges and corners so that there were no points where Karen could get snagged as she slid onto it and Rita supplied the sheepskin, which I stapled over the outside surfaces with extra padding on the top.

We took the finished product down to Karen's flat for a "test drive". The box fitted snugly over the wheelchair's right foot-rest and formed a comfortable bridge, which Karen was able to negotiate without too much trouble. Rita's simple but brilliant idea had solved a difficult problem, allowing Karen to be independent for a little while longer.

-0-0-0-0-0-

In July 2012, after suffering from several bouts of pneumonia, my dad, Frank, was admitted to the Royal Liverpool hospital, where he suffered a sudden cardiac arrest. The excellent nursing staff managed to revive him and he was stunned to hear that his heart had stopped and we had nearly lost him.

"There's nothing there, Dave," he told me at visiting time.

"Nothing where, Dad?" I asked.

"There's no heaven. It was just like having an anaesthetic and waking up again."

Frank had always been sceptical of people who claimed that, during a near-death episode, they had undergone an out-of-body experience, floating above their corpse, or had seen a blinding, white light and deceased family members beckoning them to join them. He was a confirmed unbeliever and his own heart-stopping moment only served to reinforce this belief.

His body was clearly failing but his mind was still as sharp as ever and, after his recent brush with death, he decided to sign a DNR (Do Not Resuscitate) order, insisting he was ready to go if his heart stopped again. He was placed on the controversial Liverpool Care Pathway, a palliative care scheme developed to provide high-quality, end-of-life care, and he was transferred to the Marie Curie Hospice in Woolton "to die with dignity". He was completely lucid during his last days, insisting he had enjoyed a good life and was not afraid of death. He passed away peacefully in his sleep with his family around him on Saturday 28 July 2012.

I would particularly miss my dad. We had been to almost every Liverpool home game together for more than 50 years. Also, from the age of 10, I had worked every weekend with him on his early-morning milk round and later, when he bought his first grocery shop, I would help out on the busy Saturdays, boning sides of bacon and serving customers. My dad was rough around the edges but he was a diamond, who had a great sense of humour and loved his family dearly.

-0-0-0-0-0-

Rita continued to be concerned about Karen's physical deterioration, which was due in the most part to her worsening rheumatoid arthritis. When Karen had a flare-up, she couldn't do anything for herself and, of course, Rita was always there to help. The problem was that we now lived in a house that was unsuitable for Karen so, during these flare-ups, Rita would stay at the flat, sleeping on the couch.

By January 2013, the frequency of Karen's flare-ups had increased and Rita spent a lot of nights on Karen's couch. It became clear that we needed a bungalow so that Karen could stay with us during those periods when she needed Rita's help most and, fortunately, we knew of one for sale in Greenhill Road, just around the corner from where we used to live in Melbreck Road.

Rita and I went to see the detached bungalow, which had belonged to a wheelchair-bound man and his brother. When the disabled man passed away, his brother, Peter, lived there on his own for a while but was currently living in a nursing home. The bungalow needed some tender loving care but, generally speaking, it was perfect. It was surrounded by paving, the interior doors were wide enough for a wheelchair, and it came with a large garage with a convenient ramp into the living accommodation. Two of Peter's neighbours, John Ross and Kathy Crewsdon, were selling the bungalow on Peter's behalf and, coincidentally, they were old friends of ours, so we were in pole position to buy the property.

We quickly agreed the sale and, on 24th April, we moved in, along with the builders. The interior of the bungalow was virtually gutted and rebuilt to our own specification and, two months later, we had the perfect home for us and for Karen, whenever she needed it.

On 20th April 2013, Michael celebrated his 40th birthday. Unlike his sister, he wasn't comfortable being the centre of attention and preferred to take his immediate family to Center Parcs for a long weekend in the 400-acre Whinfell Forest Village, which was situated in the picturesque Lake District National Park. Rita, Karen, and I met Mike, Joanne, Joseph, and Ben at the resort and shared a rudimentary but comfortable log-cabin-style lodge, set in stunning woodland, abounding with wildlife, including a colony of endangered red squirrels.

The central facilities included a scenic lake, where we could practice our kayaking skills before relaxing at the Lakeside Inn, the Subtropical Swimming Paradise, a series of inter-connected swimming pools with a range of steep, twisting water slides, a Sports Plaza offering a plethora of sports, including tennis, badminton, and squash, and a selection of restaurants and bars to suit every taste.

We thoroughly enjoyed the whole country park experience, looking out for the timid red squirrels on our many long walks through the forest, frolicking in the paddling pool with four-year-old Ben and enjoying the dubious thrill of the water slides with seven-year-old Joseph, watched by a beaming Auntie Karen.

Soon after we returned from our Center Parcs mini-break, Rita noticed a red area on Karen's back that looked suspiciously like the onset of a pressure sore. However, when exploring the area, Rita could feel a lump that seemed to be trying to break through the surface of the skin. Rita asked Karen to make an appointment with Dr Brookes, our family GP, who was very familiar with Karen's medical history, and he referred her to her current orthopaedic specialist, Marcus De Matas. Mr De Matas was the latest in a line of orthopaedic specialists looking after Karen since Professor Owen had retired. An x-ray confirmed that one of the surgical screws holding Karen's spinal metalwork in place had been somehow displaced and was starting to break through the skin.

Mr De Matas was one of Karen's favourite people and he, in turn, was enamoured with his patient. They would routinely spend many oblivious minutes chatting about everyday subjects like fashion and holidays before getting down to the business at hand. On this occasion, however, Marcus was subdued.

"Well, Karen," he began. "I'm afraid we are going to have to take out your bits of metal. I think replacing the rod will cause more problems than it will solve, so I think we will simply take it out before it causes more problems."

"B... b... but, what will happen to my spine when the rod is taken out? Will it bend again?" she asked.

"After all these years, I think it should be able to support itself but, over time, there might be some slight curvature. Let's worry about that if it happens. For now, we must concentrate on solving the immediate problem. We will schedule the surgery as soon as we possibly can. OK, Karen?"

Karen nodded dumbly, resigned to her fate.

Around six weeks later, at the Royal Hospital, Mr De Matas performed the surgery to remove the metalwork that had supported Karen's spine for more than thirty-five years. She recovered well after the operation and was soon discharged from the hospital. Rita and I noticed that Karen now sat differently in her wheelchair. She seemed to be leaning forward more than she had previously and it was something we would need to keep an eye on.

-0-0-0-0-0-

On 30th August 2014, we received the most devastating news. Debbie Jones (now Horwood), Karen's great friend, suddenly passed away. Debbie had married Paul Horwood many years earlier and they had two lovely boys, Scott and Thomas, whom Karen doted on. Paul walked out on Debbie when the boys were very young and it was Debbie's current partner, John, who delivered the sad news.

They had been in their caravan in North Wales when Debbie began to feel unwell. She was a long-term dialysis patient after suffering kidney failure some years earlier and was waiting for a kidney transplant. John drove the now-unconscious Debbie to Bodelwydden Hospital, where it was confirmed that she had contracted a serious infection, which had escalated into sepsis. The prognosis was grim and Debbie died a few hours later without regaining consciousness.

Karen was bereft with grief as were Rita and I, who had known Debbie since she was a young girl. Debbie had the most unique and amazing laugh and she was always laughing despite her disabilities. She would be greatly missed.

-0-0-0-0-0-

One otherwise routine day in October 2014, I suddenly experienced agonising pain in my left thigh, the one containing my latest hip implant, inserted five years previously. I went to see my GP, had a frontal x-ray, and an orthopaedic "expert" could find nothing untoward, suggesting only that I should see a specialist if the pain continued. The pain did not miraculously disappear and, in February 2015, my GP referred me to the orthopaedic trauma surgeon, Mr V Peter. He compared the latest x-ray with the x-ray taken immediately after my operation five years earlier and he spotted a small dot on the side of the implant that wasn't there before. To investigate further, he sent me for a side-on x-ray and, when he had studied the picture, he told me "The good news is I know what the problem is. The bad news is that it will be extremely difficult to fix."

He displayed the x-ray picture on a PC screen on his desk for Rita and I to see. The x-ray clearly showed that the implanted titanium hip had snapped about hallway down my thigh. How this had not shown up on the original x-ray remained a mystery.

"The top half will come out easily," Mr Peter mused. "But getting the lower piece out will be a nightmare. I will have to split the bone, remove the broken implant, insert a new one, and wire the bone back together again."

Mr Peter was based at the Liverpool Broadgreen Hospital but, because of my heart condition, he would have to perform the surgery in the Royal. It seemed I would need to be put on a heart by-pass machine during the op to relieve potential stress on my heart, and Broadgreen did not have all of the equipment he would need. He would make the arrangements and hoped to arrange the operation soon.

After several months had passed with no word from the hospital and with any movement of my left leg causing spasms of agony as the top part of the implant moved against the bone, I wrote a letter of complaint to the Medical Director of the Royal Hospital, Dr Peter Williams. On 16th September 2015, Dr Williams replied that Mr Peter was not automatically allocated theatre time at the Royal and I would need to wait for a cancellation or for a surgeon to go on holiday. He also said he would review the current standard procedures after my long wait so that anyone else in my situation would not have to wait so long in future. I would also have to wait for a High Dependency Unit bed to be available for my aftercare.

On 13th October 2015, Rita and I celebrated our 50th wedding anniversary. I was told that a guest at our wedding, who shall remain anonymous, was of the opinion that our union would not last more than a year! I love proving people wrong! However, I was in too much discomfort to celebrate with anything other than a cup of tea and a pain-killer. We would celebrate with a special cruise when I was back to full fitness.

I eventually received a letter from the Royal confirming my operation for Friday 22 January 2016. I arrived at 7:30am, was prepped for surgery, and was lying on a trolley in an ante-room next to the operating theatre, waiting for the anaesthetist to arrive. Ten minutes later, it became clear there was a problem – there was no bed available in the High Dependency Unit. The anaesthetist was apparently chasing around the hospital, cajoling, twisting arms, but still no bed was available. I was taken back to the pre-op unit and it seemed my surgery was to be cancelled. A nurse called Rita to explain the situation and, although I couldn't hear her response, from the nurse's reaction, Rita was giving her a right old earful! While this was happening, a breathless anaesthetist ran into the unit and told me he had secured the high-dependency bed and the surgery was back on. Panic over.

Seven hours later, I awoke in the recovery room and was soon transferred to the High Dependency Unit, where Rita, Karen, and Michael were anxiously waiting. I was taking self-administered morphine for the pain, clicking the button that released the shot every half-hour or so. The morphine had a weird hallucinatory effect on me and, although I have no memory of this, I apparently told Rita at visiting time on Saturday that I could see a colony of rats walking across the ceiling and there was one on the nurse's back. This caused great amusement and concern in equal measures.

My dedicated HDU nurse was a lovely Spanish guy called Jorge, the Spanish equivalent of George, and early on Monday morning, around 4am, he noticed my stats were deteriorating quickly. He was so concerned he woke up the on-call doctor to check me out and, although I was unaware at the time, he feared a pulmonary embolism was the culprit and ordered an emergency CAT scan. Fortunately, as a pulmonary embolism can be fatal, they discovered I had pneumonia in both lungs – the lesser of two evils.

After five days of intravenous antibiotics and some time spent inside a sort of see-through helmet, which was flooded with oxygen and made me look like Bart Simpson, the pneumonia cleared up and I was transferred to a private side-room in the orthopaedic ward, where Mr Peter came to see me. He told me the surgery was a great success and that this latest hip should last me a lifetime. Now where had I heard that before? Nevertheless, I was soon walking with two elbow crutches and then with one crutch. I completed all of the physiotherapy exercises, including climbing up and down stairs, and was eventually discharged, as good as new.

On Saturday 7 May 2016 we celebrated Karen's upcoming 50th birthday with a party at the local Heath Hall, where the entertainment was provided by Karl Terry and The Cruisers, a 5-piece rock 'n roll band, which included a fabulous Saxophone player. Karl, who in the early 60s was nicknamed "The Sheik of Shake" by Bob Wooler, the famous compere of the original Cavern Club, was a legend of the Mersey Beat era. Now in his late seventies and dressed in a draped teddy-boy jacket and drainpipe trousers, Karl belted out a raft of rock 'n roll classics, including my favourite Check Berry numbers, *Roll Over Beethoven*, *Sweet Little Sixteen* and *Johnny B Goode*.

The Cruisers mostly played the music of Elvis Presley, Chuck Berry, Jerry Lee Lewis, Carl Perkins, and other rock 'n roll legends of the late 50s and early 60s, which were my formative years as far as music was concerned. In 1958, aged 13, I had bought my first vinyl record, Elvis's second studio album, which included the hit records *Hound Dog*, *Don't Be Cruel*, and *That's All Right Mama*, his first Sun Records single.

I spoke to Karl during a break between sets and he told me that, during a brief period when the Cruisers split up, he had also worked with 60s legends Rory Storm & the Hurricanes, Gerry & the Pacemakers, and the Beatles. I was in exalted company!

Karen enjoyed her party so much. She loved rock 'n roll and was delighted when Karl sang Elvis's *Blue Moon of Kentucky*. As you will have realised by now, we celebrated all of Karen's landmark birthdays with a party. There were two reasons for this: the first was that Karen really loved parties when all of her close family and friends were together in one place and the second was that Rita and I were so pleased she had reached yet another milestone, we just had to make it a special occasion.

-0-0-0-0-0-

Karen's condition continued to deteriorate and Rita noticed that her breathing was shallow, perhaps because her posture had changed since the removal of the Harrington Rod. Dr Brookes checked Karen over and was concerned enough to send her straight to A&E at the Royal Hospital. Here, a doctor confirmed that Karen's oxygen levels were very low and she was transferred to a ward where she was immediately treated with a CPAP (Continuous Positive Airway Pressure) machine, which delivers pressurised air, through a tube attached to a mask, at regular intervals. After 30 minutes on the CPAP machine, Karen's improvement was incredible. Her stats were almost back to normal and she felt much better. Karen was later told that she would need to use this machine every night while sleeping.

After a few days, Karen was transferred to a special CPAP unit at Aintree Hospital, where they would determine which type of mask would suit her best. Some patients find it extremely difficult to get used to the CPAP machine but Karen managed just fine and, after a few days when she routinely slept with the mask on, she was soon discharged, along with her personal CPAP machine.

However, before the end of 2016, Karen was beset with another health worry. She had a prolapsed bowel and, because of her breathing difficulties, the specialist to whom she was referred, Dr Raj, was loathe to operate under a general anaesthetic. Instead, he tried a procedure under a local anaesthetic, which unfortunately, was not successful. Several months later he made another attempt to fix the problem under local anaesthetic, but this lasted just a few days before Karen's bowel prolapsed again. It was decided that the only way to fix it permanently was to perform a more complicated procedure with Karen closely monitored under a general anaesthetic. She would have to be assessed by a consultant anaesthetist first, but they said they would go ahead and arrange the surgery at Whiston Hospital.

Having a prolapsed bowel meant that Karen needed help every time she went to the toilet so, for convenience, she stayed with us in our bungalow, returning to her flat for a few days from time to time, with Rita again sleeping on the couch.

After using the CPAP machine for many months, Karen started coughing up blood and we took her directly to A&E to get her checked out. A scan showed that she had a pulmonary embolism in a part of her lung where it was unlikely to cause any major problems. She was prescribed a blood thinning medication – warfarin, which was first used as rat poison before being approved as a blood-thinning medication used to treat blood clots. The level of warfarin in Karen's blood would have to be carefully monitored and she would need to go for regular blood tests at a special clinic to check that the dosage was at the right level.

Karen continued to live with us and would do so until after her bowel operation. After a lengthy pre-operative assessment, her surgery was eventually scheduled for Tuesday 20th March 2018.

Twenty

Sunday 18th March 2018, Liverpool, England

On this portentous Sunday, I woke at around 8am and, as I did every Sunday, I collected my newspapers from the corner shop, had breakfast while reading the papers, and at around 11am, I decamped to my home office to check my emails. I was now semi-retired, working part-time for Michael's company, developing online IT courses and providing technical support. Rita and Karen both enjoyed a lie-in after staying up late the previous night watching television.

While I was replying to some support emails, Rita sleepily wished me good morning and went in to Karen's bedroom to wake her up and help her into her wheelchair. A few minutes later, Rita re-appeared.

"Dave, can you call the doctor, please? Karen is not feeling well. I'm just going to get her some paracetamol." Rita said, before going to the kitchen.

I popped my head into Karen's bedroom and asked if she was OK. She nodded but she was very pale and was clearly out-of-sorts. Rita returned with the paracetamol but Karen suddenly started coughing up a river of blood.

"Phone an ambulance," Rita screamed, while holding Karen and trying her best to catch the blood in a bunch of tissues.

I got through to the ambulance service almost immediately and, while I was explaining the problem, Karen's head slumped forward and she stopped breathing.

The dispatcher told me that an ambulance was on the way and in the meantime to lay Karen on her side in the recovery position. I don't know where Rita got the strength from but she heaved Karen's lifeless body out of the wheelchair and onto the bed. A first responder arrived and placed an oxygen mask over Karen's nose and mouth and used a machine to suck the blood out of her lungs. The paramedics arrived within minutes and transferred Karen into the ambulance, which roared off with its klaxons blaring. The first responder had gone with them leaving his vehicle behind.

"She's gone, Dave," Rita cried.

"They can work miracles these days so let's hope they can revive her," I replied without conviction.

We piled into Karen's van and followed in the wake of the ambulance to the Royal Hospital. We found a parking place and rushed into the A&E department. I found a nurse and asked where Karen was. She left to find out, returning a few minutes later.

"Can you please wait in the relative's room?" she asked, kindly. "One of the doctors will be in to see you shortly." She led us to the empty relative's room and my bowels suddenly turned to water.

"I'll be back in a second, Rio, I need the toilet."

Returning to the relative's room a few minutes later, I opened the door to find Rita sobbing and being comforted by a doctor and a nurse, a scene that would haunt me for many months to come.

"No, no, no!" I screamed, my voice sounding disconnected, as though it was someone else shouting and sobbing incoherently. Rita and I clung onto each other, offering whatever solace we could, both of us suffering unspeakable agony.

After the initial shock subsided, the doctor told us that they had tried for 40 minutes to revive Karen, without success, and that she would have been severely brain-damaged had she survived. The nurse then asked if we wanted to see our daughter and we followed her to the resuscitation area, where there were six bays, one of which had drapes drawn around it. The nurse pointed to the curtained bay and I pushed the drapes aside and stepped inside.

Karen was lying on her back. She was pale and there was a faint Mona Lisa smile on her blue lips, as though she were enjoying a particularly pleasant dream. Rita and I took turns hugging and kissing our lovely girl, expecting her to wake up at any second and return our embraces, before returning to the relative's room. The same kindly nurse told us that Karen's death was currently unexplained and that we would have to wait for the police to arrive to provide them with a statement.

As if in a dream, I telephoned Michael to give him the bad news. He was, of course, stunned and grief-stricken in equal measure, but he said he would come to the hospital as soon as possible. I then telephoned my brother-in-law and old friend, Chris Hammond, and asked him to ring around as many of the family as possible to let them know that our beautiful daughter had gone.

I then rang one of our oldest friends, Pauline Gill, and asked her to pass on the news to as many of our mutual friends as possible. Half-an-hour later, Pauline arrived at the hospital to support us, despite her husband, Sam, being stricken with Parkinson's Disease and requiring her constant care.

The dream-like state persisted. We went back and forth to Karen's body while waiting for the police. Michael arrived after a three-hour train journey and the outpouring of grief resumed. At around 5:30pm, five hours after we were given the devastating news, a policewoman and a young police cadet arrived.

The policewoman offered her condolences and asked me if I would give them a statement. My distraught wife was being comforted by my equally distraught son, so I was happy to comply. She asked about Karen's medical history and about what had happened on the day she died. Half-an-hour later, we were done and the policewoman accompanied me to Karen's cubicle so that I could formally identify her.

Before leaving us, the policewoman told me that the Coroner would have to be informed and that Karen's body could not be released until the Coroner was satisfied with the cause of death. I was informed that the Coroner would call me tomorrow. After saying our tearful goodbyes to

Karen, we left the hospital and drove home, still stunned, not really believing that it had happened.

It was heart-breaking to go into Karen's bedroom, where she had died so suddenly. Nothing can prepare you for the loss of a child but the suddenness of Karen's death, with no prior warning, left Rita and I both bereft and shell-shocked. It was, without doubt, the worst day of our lives and the grief was all-consuming.

That night, Rita "slept" in Karen's bed, inhaling her scent and tearfully remembering happier times. Neither of us would find sleep easy to come by for many weeks to come.

Our beloved daughter was gone.

Epilogue

At around 2pm on the day after Karen died, I received a call from a lady called Carole from the Coroner's Office. She offered her condolences and told me that there would be no need for a post mortem if Karen's GP, Dr Brookes, would sign a death certificate stating the primary cause of death as a pulmonary embolism and the secondary cause as spina bifida. She said she would call him and ring me back.

Rita and I were anxious that there should not be a post mortem. Karen's body had gone through enough trauma when she was alive and we didn't want her to be subjected to any more. Carole rang me back an hour later and confirmed that Dr Brookes would sign the death certificate and I could pick it up from his surgery the next morning. A small mercy.

There is little point in dwelling on our grief. All mothers and fathers will at least be able to imagine the depth of our torment.

Michael and I picked up the death certificate from the surgery, drove to St George's Hall in Liverpool city centre to officially report the death and to receive the certified copies of the death certificate that we would need to handle Karen's financial affairs, and drove back to Garston to arrange Karen's funeral with Thomas Porter & Sons, who had served us well in the past.

Over the course of the next week or so, we received phone calls, visits, and nearly 200 cards from family and friends who wanted to express their sympathy but didn't quite know what to say that would make things easier for us. It was enough to know that they were there. No words could change the all-consuming grief and sense of loss that we felt.

Dr Brookes, who had been Karen's GP for more than twenty years, called to offer his sympathy and to tell us what a privilege it had been for him to look after Karen. He also said that Karen could not have had two better parents and this gave us some comfort.

Rita and I visited Karen at the funeral parlour. Rita had picked out Karen's favourite dress and she looked beautiful. It was a highly distressing experience. Rita had brought one of Karen's handbags, containing a small bottle of her favourite Tia Maria coffee liqueur, which she positioned next to her in the satin-lined, white casket. This was the last time Rita would see Karen. She was so distraught that it would have been cruel for her to go through it again.

My brother, Barry, arrived from Sydney, as I suspected he would and, the day before Karen's funeral, I accompanied him to see Karen for the last time. I left some photographs and other mementos close to Karen's heart in the casket before it was closed.

The day of Karen's funeral was surreal. It was a dream-like experience that I couldn't quite believe was happening. Before the funeral, our bungalow was packed with family and friends and presently the hearse arrived carrying Karen's casket, which was adorned with a magnificent floral display, resplendent in Karen's favourite colours. Rita and I led the mourners outside and we each kissed Karen's casket before taking our places in the lead car.

As we entered the Rosemary Chapel at Springwood Crematorium, we were welcomed by one of Karen's favourite Elvis tracks, *The Wonder of You*, which I thought was rather apt. A photograph of Karen, taken on one of our cruises, was placed on top of the casket.

The service was conducted by a humanist, Bernie Olyett, who had spent an entire afternoon with Rita and I finding out all he could about Karen's life. His eulogy, which included a moving piece provided by Karen's brother, Michael, was pretty much perfect, at times heart-wrenching but often humorous.

In place of a prayer, the congregation, which numbered more than 250, with many standing in the aisles and other mourners following the service from outside, Bernie played Louis Armstrong's version of *What a Wonderful World*, which was playing on the radio at the precise moment that Karen died. Coincidently, this was also Rita's Dad's all-time favourite song. Rita and I clung to each other, our tears mingling.

The service closed with Elvis's version of *You'll Never Walk Alone*, which combined Karen's favourite singer and the anthem of her beloved Liverpool Football Club. Outside, we chatted with the mourners but, to tell the truth, it was all a bit of a blur. It was gratifying, though, to see so many people pay their respects to our wonderful daughter.

The wake was held at the Heath Hall, where hostess Jan had laid on a delicious buffet. Rita and I went from table to table, thanking everyone for coming, and reminiscing with stories of Karen's life. Especially poignant was a chat with my cousin Alan and his wife Carole who, four years earlier had lost their eldest son, Scott, aged just 38. They knew precisely how it felt for Rita and I. Alan told me that he would be lying if he told me it would get easier as time went on. "You just learn to live with it," he said.

A week later, we buried half of Karen's ashes in my mum and dad's grave, retaining the other half for scattering in the places that Karen loved most in the world. Michael will scatter some of Karen's remains beneath the Hollywood sign in Los Angeles during his forthcoming holiday. Karen's friend, Pat Adair, will scatter some in Las Vegas and another friend, Pauline Reilly, will leave a small part of Karen forever in New York City. The remainder, Rita and I will scatter into the wake of the Britannia cruise ship as it passes through the Straits of Gibraltar.

-0-0-0-0-0-

The precise cause of spina bifida is still a mystery. Scientists suspect that the biggest contributory factor to spina bifida is a lack of folic acid (vitamin B9) in the mother's diet and, today, expectant mothers typically take folic acid supplements, which is thought to prevent 7 out of 10 cases of spina bifida. It is still not known how folic acid helps prevent spina bifida but its thought that vitamin B9 is required for important biochemical reactions in the mother's body.

In those cases where folic acid doesn't prevent spina bifida, modern scans detect the condition at a very early stage and many such pregnancies are routinely terminated. So, the number of special children like Karen is greatly reduced. I like to think that, had we known that Karen would be born with spina bifida at an early stage of Rita's pregnancy and we had been offered a termination, we would have chosen not to terminate. But, who knows? Obviously, we would have preferred Karen not to have spina bifida but a termination would have robbed the world of an extraordinary life and deprived us of the pleasure of bringing up such a wonderful daughter.

Rita and I were happy that Karen had enjoyed as "normal" a life as possible given her circumstances. She achieved most of her ambitions. For many years, she had a job she loved, she had her own specially-adapted transport, and she lived in a purpose-built flat. She visited Graceland, flew to Singapore and Australia, holidayed in New York, Las Vegas, and Los Angeles, met many of her Liverpool Football Club idols, enjoyed cruises around the Mediterranean, the Canary Islands, and the Baltic Sea, to name just a few, and generally enjoyed life to the full.

One final comment. As far as I am concerned, Rita is a leading candidate for "The Greatest Mum... Ever!" award. She was only seventeen when she gave birth to Karen but she instinctively knew what was best for our daughter and I am extremely proud of her. I had done my best to help Karen, of course, but there are certain things that only a mum can help with. Rita was not just Karen's mum. She was her friend and carer and Karen's passing has left a big hole in her life that will never again be filled.

Printed in Poland
by Amazon Fulfillment
Poland Sp. z o.o., Wrocław

52732421R00179